The
Lory Owners
Survival Guide

Margrethe Warden

Mindo Press, LLC
Danielsville, Pennsylvania
18038

Front cover art, rear cover art, and Lory tongue drawing by
Gamini Ratnivira and used herein with permission.

Drawing by Mark Ziembicki is used
herein with permission.

Cover and book design by Russell W. Shade

ISBN # 0-9747971-1-1

Published in the United States by
Mindo Press, LLC.
3724 Filbert Drive,
Danielsville PA 18038-9754

For Mary in New Jersey

May you always have joy and red birds in your life.

And

In memory of Ozzie and Chirpy and maybe a tiny bit to the Demonic Dusky.

Contents

Chapter 3
BREEDING LORIES   73

Chapter 4
LORIES IN
HEALTH AND SICKNESS   85

Chapter 5
FREQUENTLY ASKED QUESTIONS   131

Chapter 6
LORIES – THE FAMILY LORIIDAE   143

References   177

Index   181

FOREWORD

I was more than happy when asked to write a foreword to this excellent and comprehensive book. The Lory Owner's Survival Guide is a very necessary tool, especially for the new or would be lory owner as well those of us that have been involved with these remarkable birds for some time.

Personally, I've been breeding birds for over 30 years and most of those years have included lories. In the early days there was little or no information available on these wonderful parrots. We knew they had a specialized diet, but what was it? Lory keepers had their own "perfect" concoction, which they were loath to share with others. It's amazing that the birds survived as well as they did with our venture into witchcraft in order to feed them.

Lory breeders would descend upon a quarantine station just as soon as USDA released the birds in hopes of finding that rare specimen that somehow got mixed in with the more common species. And find them we did! Josephine's mixed in with the Stella's, Rosenberg's mixed with Green-napeds.

It was a lory lover's paradise in those days. Lories of many, many species were available and at reasonable prices. Little did we know at the time that our days in paradise were numbered.

Those days are long gone, as are many of the lory species that we enjoyed working with. Why? Why, because in some cases we didn't know enough about what we were doing with dietary needs, housing requirements or too many babies of rare species were sent off to the pet trade. Of course in those days we thought that the supply of lories being imported was unending, if you lost a breeder, you just purchased one from the next shipment, as there was always a next shipment. No more!

Now that we no longer have free access to wild caught lories it's all the more important that we offer proper care for those in our trust. Today's pet might well be tomorrow's breeder.

Since those free wheeling days we've learned a lot, especially as it comes to diets and diseases that affect lories. We've learned which species are easier to breed, which ones make the better pets or make the better talkers. Which ones don't make good companion birds at all.

Little by little all of this information has been gathered together. There are now lory societies, including international ones. There are lory symposiums that deal with all aspects of lory keeping. Look at the Internet, several email lists just for lory folks. Wonderful information is being handed out by all of us concerned with the future and well being of these special parrots. This informative and very necessary book has been authored by one of the most visible people in the lory world today, Margrethe Warden. It has been my pleasure to know Margrethe for many years and to discuss many aspects of our feathered charges. She has delved deep into the world of diets and diseases. Of what makes a good pet and what does not. She has worked tirelessly to promote the proper care of lories and is a font of information on the Internet.

There have been many books written on the subject of lories, some better than others. This is a keeper.

Dick Schroeder
Escondido, California
March, 2004

ACKNOWLEDGEMENTS

It hasn't been that many years since that first lory captured my heart and sent my life in an unexpected direction, from civil servant to aviculturist. While I do not claim to be an expert on lories, I have learned a lot since then and would like to share my experiences with others. It's been an interesting journey and changed me forever. Of all the changes that have taken place as a result, the most significant has been the many wonderful people that were brought into my life.

It takes a lot of people to put together a book. The Lory Owner's Survival Guide would not have been possible without the assistance of a number of extraordinary individuals. At the top of that list are Mary and Frank Chinnici of Neptune, NJ, who were responsible for forcing me to get the project off the ground and providing ongoing encouragement as I undertook the writing process. Their love of lories and their experiences, both joyful and heartbreaking, provided much of the inspiration I needed. They have helped me learn more about lories and insisted there was a need for this type of book. Mary, along with, Brenda Piper and Dick Schroeder, were invaluable with their help in reading sections, offering advice, information, suggestions, and general support and encouragement. Their input was not only greatly appreciated; it was also incorporated into many pages of this book. Sandee Molenda provided some additional input and insight; Matt Schmit contributed some of his wisdom as well. Unless otherwise noted, all photographs in this book were taken by me. Kristen Bliss of Michigan, who didn't know me from Adam's house cat, not only gave me permission to use a picture of her Green-naped Lory, Stitch, she also graciously offered to take more pictures for me to use. Likewise, Richard Brancato was willing to let me use photographs of his Duyvenbode's Lory Squirt. Exceptional wildlife artist, Gamini Ratnivira of Fallbrook, CA, provided a sketch of a lory tongue and offered the use of his beautiful lory images as the cover design. Trevor Buckell of England and Gert van Dooren of the Netherlands helped me with information on lories kept in Europe and elsewhere. My friend Sheldon Dingle, in a moment of insanity, offered to proofread and edit the manuscript. His job may well have been more difficult than the actual writing! Dick Schroeder and Donna Lynn Salyer each did a final proof read, just in case. And I am certainly glad they did. Any mistakes that appear in this book are my own.

Since I began keeping birds I have been fortunate to have had access to some of the best avian vets in the country. They include William Olkowski of Cedarcrest Animal Hospital in Fishersville, VA; Cheryl Greenacre of the University of Tennessee and Branson Ritchie and Heather Wilson of the University of Georgia. They have taught me a lot and the knowledge I have gained from them appears in this book. The health and illness parts of this book are meant only to be a basic reference and I do not intend for this to be a medical text or a replacement for veterinary care. I am not a vet, never will be a vet and do not want to give the impression that this is all the medical information you will ever need.

I'm also grateful for the several Internet e-mail lists that, over the years, have provided me with a great education. The learning process is reflected in this book.

Chapter 1
INTRODUCTION TO LORIES

Lories, also called lorikeets, are a unique group of parrots that have gained popularity in the Unites States. The Loriinae family members are brush-tongued parrots that hail from Australia and the South Pacific. Being some of the most brightly colored members of the parrot world, these birds are unique in many ways. Not only are their colors more brilliant than most of their psittacine relatives, their dietary requirements are completely different. The lory tongue is covered with little brushes called papillae. These enable the birds to collect pollen, which, along with fruits and nectar, comprises the largest portion of their diet. They do not collect nectar in the neat and gentle fashion of hummingbirds; they tend to crush the flowers and consume the nectar and pollen, making them less than popular in agricultural environments. They do not eat hard foods and seeds like other parrots, and it has been noted that their ventriculus (gizzard) is not strong enough to process many of those items.

Since the 1990s, lories have gained popularity as both pets and aviary birds. They have earned their place in aviculture as some of the most delightful and desirable parrots.

What Is Aviculture?

Webster's defines Aviculture as "the raising and care of birds and especially of wild birds in captivity." It is also considered the captive husbandry of wild birds or simply as the keeping and raising of birds. In the broad sense of the word, all of us who keep birds are aviculturists. The keeping of exotic birds has become quite popular in the last forty or so but it is by no means a modern occurrence. It is documented that birds have been kept as far back as 6000 years ago in ancient Egypt. Birds were revered and some were even considered gods. Mummified birds were found in tombs because it was believed that upon death, the human soul turned into a bird. The Egyptians were not alone in the love for birds. Ancient Chinese and Phoenicians kept birds as depicted in their artifacts. The Greeks found parrots to be charming and interesting birds and were apparently the first to collect them. When Alexander the Great conquered the Persian Empire 2700 years ago in 333 B. C., he brought Alexandrine Parakeets and other birds into Europe, where they became quite popular. The Incas kept Amazon Parrots and renderings of a variety of birds show up in their artifacts. Montezuma had what were probably the first walk-through aviaries and they encompassed ten rooms filled with thousands of birds including parrots, wrens, hummingbirds and birds of prey. In 1521, Cortez set fire to the aviaries. More recently, as explorers and adventurers traveled to those strange and faraway places over the last few hundred years, they brought beautiful native birds back with them. Columbus returned to Spain with a pair of parrots and many others did likewise. As those at home saw the beautiful inhabitants of these remote places, the love affair with birds continued to develop. Success in breeding birds is evident back several hundred years B.C. when the Chinese were raising gamecocks for the sport of fighting. While illegal in many places and often viewed with horror, this sport's history spans thousands of years from the Ancient Middle East to modern America. Both the first and third Presidents of the United States raised gamecocks for fighting.

U.S. Presidents also kept the kinder, gentler types of birds as well. Martha Washington is reported to have had a pet parrot named Polly, however, there is some indication her husband detested it. Thomas Jefferson's preference was for mockingbirds. James Madison had a parrot. During the War of 1812, Dolly Madison's parrot was rescued from the White House. Ulysses S. Grant had chickens and a parrot; Rutherford Hayes, Grover Cleveland, and Warren Harding had canaries. Theodore Roosevelt brought birds, at least one of which was a blue macaw, into the White House with him in 1901. Harry Truman began the custom of pardoning a Thanksgiving turkey although it may actually have been Abraham Lincoln who issued the first "pardon" to his own pet turkey, Jack. The most recent Presidential birds were Lyndon Johnson's lovebirds.

Although mankind has been keeping birds for thousands of years, the reasons for keeping them vary. In some cases, such as falcons and game-cocks, birds are kept for sport. Some cultures kept birds because they were tied into their religious or spiritual beliefs. Some cultures kept them for companions. Often, various types of birds were kept for food. Some birds, especially parrots, were kept because they were an indication of opulence or social status.

Brilliantly colored parrots have shared their lives with humans for years. In 1836, Victorian scientist Sir William Jardine devoted an entire volume of his 40 book series "The Naturalists Library" to parrots. Poet and author Edward Lear, of "The Owl and The Pussycat" fame, provided many of the illustrations for this book. In his 1896 book, St. George Mivart describes the beauty and personality of various lories.

In the Twentieth Century, aviculture became more popular. Jean Delacour (1890 – 1985) has often been considered to be the "father of aviculture." In the first half of the century, aviculturists such as The Duke of Bedford (1888-1953) made their mark by not only keeping and breeding many types of birds with great success but also by publishing books on the subject. These books described the characteristics of the birds and gave information on feeding, housing, and maintaining them. During the second half of the Twentieth Century, avicultural greats such as John Stoodley, Rick Jordan, Richard Schubot, and Rosemary Low added their contributions, sharing their wealth of knowledge and experience through talks and writing.

A big advancement for aviculture, occurring in the later half of the Twentieth Century was the development of methods for accurately sexing birds; first was surgical sexing in the 1970's and then the capability to determine sex using the DNA from a small sample of blood. Since so many birds were not sexually dimorphic (could not tell the difference just by looking at them), setting up true pairs included a lot of guessing and hoping and a bit of luck. With some of the larger birds especially, putting birds together for breeding could be a very expensive gamble. As a result, breeding exotic birds was not something easily undertaken by those with limited budgets. The ability to easily determine gender finally took the guesswork out of breeding parrots and other birds, making it easier to set up true pairs. With sexing made simple, aviculture became less risky and more accessible to everyone.

Getting To Know Lories

Because lories have a diet unlike other parrots, their droppings are a little wetter than what we see with other birds. For years this trait kept lories from becoming popular as pets. Overcoming the poop problem is easy and will be discussed in detail in the next chapter. All one needs is a little creativity.

Most lories can become accomplished talkers and mimics. Although they are some of the most desirable pets, those in the *Chalcopsitta* genus seem to be the least likely to verbalize, but many do. Little is known about the life expectancy of

Yellow-streaked Lory

lories, but with good diet and care, it is not unreasonable to expect your pet lory to live fifteen to twenty years.

Lories are the clowns of the parrot world. They tend to be far more active and animated than other pet birds. They are constantly on the go. They enjoy a variety of toys, both hanging and loose on the cage bottom. They also tend to be a bit excitable, especially during play, and as a result can

deliver the occasional painful nip. They are naturally inquisitive. Their curious nature makes it
easy to introduce them to different things in their
environment, such as toys and new kinds of foods.
Lories also are bold and fearless. Because they
are assertive and often aggressive, they are not
usually suitable playmates for other birds. Use
caution and vigilant supervision when placing a
lory with other species. They will charge after a
bird that is more than twice their size, and their
aggression towards other birds can result in serious injury or death. They are lightening quick
and tragedy can happen in the blink of an eye.
They will also think nothing of approaching the
family cat or dog, regardless of the size or
temperament.Their brazen personality makes up
so much of their charm, but that very thing, along
with the poop issue, are reasons why lories are
not always the best choice for a first-time bird
owner.Your lory will be an extremely active bird;
so the larger the cage, the happier the bird. Exercise will keep your bird healthy. Along with roomy
cages, play gyms are great for lories. They love
swings, things that make noise, and loose items
that they can toss about the cage.

Lories have a diet that is quite different than
most parrots and this will be discussed in greater
detail in the section on Diet. Because they mainly
consume nectar, pollen, and fruit, they need a
completely different type of food. There are several commercial lory diets available. Favorite foods
include a wide assortment vegetables and fresh
fruits. Always be sure your lory has plenty of fresh,
clean water.

Lories are susceptible to the same diseases and ailments that other parrots are. They can suffer from beak and feather disease, polyoma, gout, fatty liver, aspergillosis, and all the usual avian disorders. In addition to the common ailments, lories appear to be a group that has become vulnerable to hemochromatosis, also known as iron storage disease. Less is known about the health issues of lories than other psittacines, making it even more important for owners to have a necropsy performed when they encounter the death of one.

One final note - Lories are parrots. They are wild creatures, not having lived with humans long enough to become domesticated. They are expensive. They are time consuming. They can be quite messy. They have been known to be loud. Having a parrot will be an experience that is quite different than having a cat or dog. Birds are not for everyone.

Choosing The Lory That's Right For You

There are at least 50 known lory species, and quite a few subspecies, but not all of them occur in American aviculture. And not all the lories that do appear in aviculture show up in the pet bird trade. The most popular pet lories seem to be the ones referred to as "Rainbow Lories." Of the group of "Rainbows," the most common and nominate species is the Green-naped Lory, *Trichoglossus haematodus haematodus*. The most distinctive trait about this particular rainbow lory is the red breast feathers with dark blue edging. The other fairly common rainbow lory is the Swainson's, or Blue-mountain Lory, *T. h. moluccanus*. Another brightly colored and popular lory is the Dusky Lory, *Pseudeos fuscata*. These birds are similar in size to the rainbows. Extremely popular as a pet is the Red Lory, *Eos bornea*. Once you see this brilliant red bird it's not hard to understand why so many are drawn to it. And for those partial to red birds, there is also the Blue-streaked Lory, *Eos reticulata*. It has the same bright red plumage as its cousin the red lory but with quite a bit more blue. Of similar size and equally as striking in appearance are the Chattering Lories, *Lorius garrulus*. A group of lories that seem to make interesting pets are those in the *Chalcopsitta* genus. These include the Blacks, Duyvenbode's, and the Yellow-streaks. They are larger than the lories described above. In my own experience, they also appear to be a bit calmer and less likely to become nippy. They are somewhat more expensive than most lories, but the increased demand for them has caused their numbers to grow and the price to come down a bit

For so long the focus was on the negative aspects of lories, and their numerous good qualities were completely overlooked. Finally, this wonderful group of birds is becoming more popular and is receiving the recognition it deserves. This is in part a direct result of the popularity of bird clubs, bird conventions and seminars, and the widespread use of the Internet. In the beginning, I was unfamiliar with their diet and care and learned the hard way – by trial and error. Now the Internet provides vast resources on lories, and most information is simply an e-mail away. I stumbled onto these birds quite by accident. I met a Red Lory in a pet store, and not only was I drawn to the absolute beauty of the bird; I was also totally smitten with his personality. When I obtained that first lory, a fellow parrot owner was mortified. She told me I was insane and that lories were disgusting and only belonged in zoos. She could not have been more incorrect. That first lory was the most dynamic and entertaining parrot I had ever seen. He mastered almost every sound in his environment and entertained his human observers for hours on end. Anyone who finds these brightly colored parrots enchanting and tempting will be rewarded for many years to come. They can be affectionate and loving birds. You cannot select a more interesting or exciting bird for a companion.

Getting Your Lory

Now that you've made the decision to get a lory there are several factors to consider. From where will you get this bird and from whom? How will it arrive? What will you do with it after it arrives?

A good place to start would be with a reputable breeder. There are great people all over the United States and beyond who work with lories and one of them has the type you are looking for. You can find lory breeders through listings in magazines, bird organizations and on the Internet. Start with getting references and asking around. If the breeder provides you with names of previous customers, contact them! Ask all the questions you can think of about the breeder and about the birds. Ask other people not listed as references as well because people are not going to give out the names of unsatisfied customers. There is a large network of "lory people" out there. Find them. They are in your community, involved in the local bird club and on the Internet. Not only can they give you information about certain breeders, they can also give you information about providing the best care for your new bird. When you locate a breeder, talk to them and be sure to ask questions. Ask about diet, health, biosecurity, housing and anything else you can think of. A good breeder will be happy to answer your questions and help you to educate yourself.

You may find a pet store that offers lories for sale. There are a lot of pros and cons of buying a bird from a retail establishment. Not every pet store, even the large chain stores, know or care about feeding a lory correctly. Many often do not understand the dietary needs of lories and some will make no effort to learn. Other stores will make every effort to feed them appropriately. Sometimes stores that sell birds exclusively will be more knowledgeable and have more choices as far as food, cages and toys. If you buy a lory from a pet store you will most likely pay much more than you would buying directly from a breeder. Birds being sold in pet stores may have more opportunities to be exposed to disease than birds from breeders. If the store staff cannot tell you for sure what kind of lory it is please do not buy the bird from them.

Once you have decided where you will get your bird, you will need to settle on price, payment method, and the terms of purchase. It does not hurt to check around and find out the current market price for your particular lory; and remember that, depending on the type of lory, the price ranges from very reasonable to very expensive. Many good breeders have sales contracts that outline their responsibilities and yours. These contracts usually provide for a health guarantee based on your own vet examining the bird upon its arrival. The agreement should also outline under what conditions, if any, your money can be refunded if the bird is ill or dies soon after its arrival.

You need to know how your lory will be coming to you. If the breeder lives close enough you might be able to arrange to pick it up or to meet partway. If it is coming from out of state, the bird will probably have to be shipped via airline cargo. This would necessitate a trip to your local airport. Many airlines do not ship live animals so it's important to know what airlines fly into your area. The most common live animal carriers seem to be Continental, Delta, Alaska Airlines, and US Airways. Shipping is not usually very stressful for the bird but it can be a very difficult time for the worried new owner. Once the bird is placed inside a shipping container, it usually remains fairly calm in that dark environment. If the bird needs to change planes in transit, make sure the shipper allows sufficient time between flights to make that change. Plan to spend anywhere form $85 - $150 for the cost of shipping. Some shippers will use the US Postal Service because the price is less than commercial airlines. The Postal Service is not a recommended shipper as they may bump the bird in favor of more important cargo and it is also illegal to ship parrots with them.

Before your bird arrives, you will need to locate a good avian vet if you do not already have one. Again, your network of bird people will help you with this task. It's important that the vet be knowledgeable about birds and avian medicine and hopefully has experience with lories. When you've established an arrival date for your bird, make an appointment with the vet for a Well Bird check up. Many health guarantees require the vet check be done within three working days from arrival. Some of the basic tests include a fecal gram stain, a CBC (complete blood count), and a chemistry panel. These will give the vet a snapshot of the bird's health as well as provide a baseline for future reference.

Now that you know you will be getting this bird soon you will also need to have a suitable cage and food available. The minimum cages size in one is one in which the bird can fully outstretch its wings and be able to turn completely around. Lories use a lot of their cage space, including the top and bottom and all four sides so this is a situation where size DOES matter. The bar spacing should be narrow enough that the bird cannot get its head stuck. This cage should be one that is easily cleaned. Removable grates on the bottom and slide-out trays are important. Many owners worry about the mess caused by the runny droppings that are typical of lories. This mess can be managed simply. Plastic chair mats, seed guards, shower curtains, and other products of your ingenuity can provide protection for your walls, furniture, and carpet. Seed guards, if available, can be helpful although they do stick out and can snag clothing. An inexpensive shower curtain can be hung behind the cage to catch those squirts and thrown fruit and can be easily removed and cleaned. Panels made of acrylic or similar material can be attached to the cage and removed for cleaning. Along with the cage you will need to consider toys. Lories are active and love to play. They enjoy swings and toys they can hang from or undo. They don't chew to the degree other parrots do but they enjoy chipping away at wooden toys. One need not spend a fortune on toys either as pretty much everything is a toy to a lory.

Another thing you need to have ready for your bird's arrival is appropriate food. Lories do not eat the same diet as other parrots. They eat primarily fruit and nectar. A good commercial lory diet is very important as are a variety of fresh foods. Have the food available prior to the bird's arrival. Also, ask the seller what type of diet the bird was fed. If different from what you plan to feed, ask that they include some of its normal food when they send the bird to you. You are now ready to pick up your new lory!

Chapter 2
LORY CARE AND MAINTENANCE

Feeding Lories

There are probably as many ways to feed lories as there are people feeding them. While there is no absolute one way to feed them there are some guidelines that can make the diet quandary easier.

Lories are physiologically different than other parrots and are designed to consume a diet of nectar, pollen, fruit, bugs and such. Their brush tongue is perfectly suited to the gathering of nectar and pollen. Their ventriculus, or gizzard, is less muscular than that of other parrots thus they should not eat the hard, dry diet we feed our other parrots.

Nectar And Powder

Most lory owners and breeders have found that the birds are healthier, happier, and longer-lived when they have nectar in their diet. There are several commercial products on the market in the United States designed specifically for lories. These products are available in a dry, powdered form that should be mixed with water to make nectar. The products that are intended to be converted into liquid nectar are not suitable for long term feeding as a dry product. The ingredients are water-soluble and as a result, are more expensive than a powder meant specifically to be fed dry. Several of these products have been around since the mid 1980s and have been used extensively on flocks of lories for several generations of birds. There are also commercial lory diets available in Europe and elsewhere. If commercial nectar makes up a portion of your lory's diet there is no need to worry about adding vitamin or mineral supplements.

Because it is mixed in water, nectar should not be left out for long periods of time, as it can become a breeding ground for bacteria. If the lory lives in an environment that has low humidity and is climate controlled, the nectar will remain stable for a while but should not be left for more than twenty four hours. If the birds are housed outdoors, especially in warm and humid climates such as Texas and Florida, the nectar should be removed after just a couple of hours. Once you have become accustomed to feeding the lory it will be easy to gauge just how much the bird will consume during a certain period of time. Only feed them what they will eat and you will eliminate waste and the potential for contamination.

In the United States, Avico's Lory Life® makes a product similar in nutritional value to the nectar mix but is designed to be fed dry. The ingredients are less expensive because they do not need to be water-soluble. In fact, when mixed with water, it turns into a rather unsightly green mud. While unappetizing to humans, the lories do not seem to mind the appearance. Because lories enjoy blending things together, do not expect the powder to remain clean and uncontaminated for more then 24 hours at a time. Be sure to replace it, using a clean bowl, once it has been fouled by pieces of food or feces. If a dry diet is preferable, be sure to use one that is prepared for and tested on lories. Avoid those homemade recipes that may be nutritionally incomplete. Prior to the creation and subsequent improvement of commercial lory diets, the feeding process was rather hit or miss. Those keeping lories often created their own diet using ingredients such as dry pancake mix, rice, milk, brown sugar, flour, honey, soaked or buttered wheat bread, and sponge cake. Most early diets included the use of fruits, vegetables, flowers, and sprouted seeds. At least one text suggested offering strips of bacon in the winter for extra fat. Some of the diets given to lories were so atrocious that it is amazing any of them survived.

Fruits & Vegetables
While commercial diets are often promoted as "total nutrition," your birds will benefit from the

addition of fresh fruits and vegetables. Some of
the best items to offer a lory include papaya, can-
taloupe, mango, pears, apples, berries, sweet
potatoes, guavas, carrots, broccoli, squashes, bell
peppers, green beans, corn in moderation, peas,
jalapeno peppers, and dark leafy greens such as
kale and dandelion. Many lories love seedless
green grapes although they ought not be offered
in copious quantities as they are not as nutritious as many other fruits. Because cooking foods
destroys many of the nutrients, fresh produce
should be fed raw or only barely cooked.

Frozen vegetables can also be very nutritious as
they are normally frozen soon after they are har-
vested and do not sit in coolers or warehouse for
any length of time. Some canned items can be
nutritious; however, they should be rinsed before serving. Chopping or dicing allows you to
offer a variety of food without the problems of

the bird selecting only the morsels it's in the mood for that day. Variety is the key to feeding fresh foods. Offer a variety of fresh foods daily rather than just one or two items. An assortment of foods not only gives the bird some relief from the monotony of cage dwelling but also offers a wide range of nutrients that will help keep it happy and healthy.

Sprouts

Freshly sprouted seeds are an excellent source of vitamins, minerals, protein, enzymes and anti-oxidants. When seed begin to sprout they are at their peak nutritional level and they are easy to digest. Because they are soft, they are suitable for lory consumption. Avoid sprouts purchased in the store as they may be older and less nutritious and they can contain harmful levels of *E. coli.* Seeds and beans to include in your sprout mix are: sunflower seeds, pumpkin seeds, mung beans, wheat berries, lentil, adzuka beans, and corn.

Live Food

Some lories enjoy the occasional insect although they do not need an insect supplement to their diet. However, during breeding season, live foods such as mealworms can be added to the diet for extra protein. I had a pair of Iris Lories who loved mealworms any time but most of the others did not care much for them. Other people have indicated Goldies and Duskies also enjoyed them. If the goal is to increase the protein consumption, especially when there are chicks in the nest, but you are not excited with the live insect idea, there are some nice mixes with dried insects that can be sprinkled in the powder or over the fresh fruits and vegetables. One note on the protein however, is that unless the birds are preparing to breed, the protein levels do not need to be increased.

The Pellet Issue

Pellet manufacturers have realized the benefit of marketing species-specific diets and in doing so have jumped on the lory bandwagon. Vets often recommend a totally pelleted diet for feeding caged birds, and those who do will generally recommend them for lories as well. The commercial diet Lory Life® was formulated with the nutritional needs of lories in mind and extensively tested on large numbers of lories before being made available to the public. The manufacturer also adjusted the formulation to lower the iron content in response to concerns from lory owners. It is apparent that the same efforts have not been made on behalf of many pelleted lory diets. These pelleted diets seem to advertise that in feeding them, the lory droppings will be much firmer and will therefore eliminate some of the mess associated with keeping lories. Clearly they are designed for the consumer who looks for convenience and ease when feeding lories, not for the welfare and benefit of the birds themselves. Most experienced lory keepers will recommend that pellets be omitted from your lory's diet although some have indicated great success using them in their feeding regimen. Lories seem to prefer their pellets soaked before feeding. If you feel you want to include pellets, use one that is specifically manufactured to be low in iron.

Foods To Avoid

Human food with preservatives and added iron (ferrous sulfate) such as canned fruit, non-organic baby foods and nectar drinks intended for human consumption; chocolate; products with caffeine such as coffee, tea and soft drinks, alcohol, eggplant foliage, and the stems and leaves of tomato plants which can contain toxic levels of solanine and alkaloids that can effect calcium absorption; corn, while not toxic, is full of sugar and carbohydrates which can help bring on obesity in your bird if fed in large quantities; mushrooms; the pits of *Prunus* species (peach, apricot, cherry, plum); tobacco. There is some controversy surrounding the use of avocado. Some state it is toxic to birds however there seems to be a lack of conclusive information to support the claim. Some seem to think that the skin and pits are toxic while the flesh is safe. Some have fed avocado to their birds with no ill effects. When in doubt, err on the side of caution. At the price of avocadoes, they don't need to be fed to birds anyway.

Water

Even though your lory gets fresh nectar it is important to give it fresh, clean drinking water daily as well. The water can be delivered either in a bowl or through a water bottle. If you use water bottles they do need to be cleaned and changed daily. While there may still be water in it, it rarely remains clean for twenty four hours. When us-ing water bottles, be sure to check the tubes daily as the bird might block them by placing food or other items in the opening. If you use a water bowl do not be surprised or offended if your lory decides to use it as a bathtub. The more dry pow-der you add to the diet, the more water your lory is apt to drink. Clean water is essential to its con-tinued good health.

Cages

For any bird the housing is important. At the bare minimum, the cage should be large enough that if the bird sits in the center and stretches its wings out it could turn completely around with-out touching the sides of the cage. It should also be tall enough that the bird can perch comfort-ably at several levels without bumping its head.

The placement of the cage is as important as the cage itself. While your lory needs to be housed in an area where it has plenty of company and interaction from its human companions, the cage should not be in the area that sees the heaviest traffic. If people are constantly darting around corners and zipping on front of the cage, the bird will be startled, even frightened, many times dur-ing the day. On a constant basis, this could lead to some behaviors such as lunging, biting or fear-fulness that might be problematic. Your lory also needs plenty of sleep – ten or twelve hours of it in a dark and quiet place. If your lory is housed in a main living area where the human activity starts early in the morning and last until late at night,

consider setting up a sleeping cage in a more remote location. Sleeping cages need not be very
large nor do they need lots of toys and accessories. Your lory goes into its sleeping cage in the
evening and comes out again in the morning when

Cardinal Lory

household activity starts. If your lory is not getting sufficient rest, behavior problems can occur.

There are several factors that will influence cage selection. Price is a big one. It is easy to spend considerably more on the cage than was spent on the bird. The location of the cage is another, lesser factor. In what room it will be placed may determine certain elements such as color. Available space is a big consideration when purchasing a cage for your pet bird. While one might want to buy the biggest cage on the market, if the space available is only a 24-inch corner in the living room, the cage cannot be larger.

Lories are incredibly active birds. Unlike many other types of parrots they tend to utilize the entire cage, including top, bottom and all sides. This can present a dilemma for the person who wants a reasonably sized cage to put in their home. The ideal size for a single lory would be in the range of two feet tall, three feet wide, and three feet deep. Lories need the width and length more than the height. Unfortunately, cage manufacturers are not often inclined to make a cage with these dimensions. In the absence of other choices, look for a cage that is about twenty four inches square. If appearance is not the most important thing, breeder style cages made from galvanized wire can be larger without costing a lot. These would be the least expensive cages available.

Some lory owners have found that the dual level ferret cages work well for their lories. These cages are generally inexpensive and lightweight and they have sufficient space for the bird to move about naturally and play.

Another essential cage element is bar spacing. Make sure the bars are not far enough apart for the bird to get its head stuck. If your lory is one of the smaller varieties such as a Rainbow or Goldie's, perhaps ¾" spacing would be the safest. For the larger birds such as the *Lorius* and *Chalcopsitta* varieties, 1" spacing is acceptable. The bars must be such that toys and perches can be fastened to them securely.

Regardless of the size cage you chose, be sure the doors and feeding areas can be closed securely and your lory cannot open them. Lories are notorious escape artists and seem to spend a great deal of time plotting ways to let themselves out of the confines of a cage. A lory on the loose with its owner unaware is a lory destined for trouble or, worse, an accident. If the little Houdini is housed in an outdoor aviary without a safety area, escape can mean gone forever.

Finally, and perhaps one of the most important considerations, is cleaning and sanitizing your lory's cage. Lories, like most parrots, are not especially neat creatures. Having a pull-out bottom tray is practical. The tray can be lined with newspaper, which is cheap and safe, and can easily be removed and replaced. Most newspaper ink is vegetable based and will not harm your lory. Bedding, such as corncob or nutshells, can be unsafe. They can cause crop impaction if ingested, and the bedding itself can become a fertile breeding ground for aspergillosis.

A grate in the bottom is also a good idea as it keeps the bird out of dropped food and feces. Pull-out grates are wonderful because they can be removed and easily cleaned. The cage itself should not be so heavy that it cannot be moved easily. If a wheeled stand is available for the cage that is even better. This makes moving a bulky cage easier, even to the point of being able to wheel it outside for a good cleaning with a garden hose. Some cages also offer seed guards or some sort of attachable apron. These can be effective in catching droppings and food but be sure they can be removed easily for cleaning. Toys and perches should be those that are easily removed and cleaned. Many cage accessories such as perches and toys can be cleaned in the dishwasher.

Because the nature of lory droppings is a bit unlike other parrots you may wish to do some additional mess control. A plastic chair mat, sold in any office supply store, can protect carpets. Shower curtains or shower board can be hung on the walls behind the cage. Some people prefer to hang panels made of acrylic or similar material that can be removed for easy clean up. All you need is a little creativity and possibly a power tool.

Toys

Because these birds are active and easily entertained, providing sufficient and appropriate toys is rather simple. Lories play with great enthusiasm and to them, pretty much anything and everything can be turned into a toy. There are some necessary precautions when obtaining or making toys for your lory. If you are using any items that have ropes or fibers, monitor the condition constantly. The fraying areas can become dangerous as the fibers can get wrapped around a toe, foot, or neck. Consider the size and open spaces of the potential toy and the accompanying hardware. Would they be of a size where a lory can get its head or foot stuck? When selecting toys for your lory, also keep in mind that they can see in color so go ahead and get that really flashy one you were wondering about.

To start with, lories enjoy loose objects on the bottom of their cages. These can be plastic balls, sections cut from a cardboard paper towel tube, little whiffle balls with bells, plastic containers and tops, even plastic key rings from the infant section of the supermarket. Another favorite floor toy is a small plastic bottle, preferably with a screw-on top, filled with beads or something that makes noise and rattles when moved. Noise, and lots of it, is essential to the well being of any lory.

Next, there must be hanging toys fastened to the top of the cage. Most lories enjoy swings. You can obtain an actual bird swing with a PVC, wooden, or concrete perching area or you can fashion your own using a little imagination. Again, use caution if you are using rope as it can easily become frayed. While lories don't have the destructive chewing habits that other psittacines have, they do enjoy some softer wooden items and they will demolish them. Because lories enjoy the challenge of dismantling things, rawhide knots can be another source of amusement. You must also be careful about the fastening hardware you use to attach the toy to the cage. Lories love a challenge and will enjoy undoing and removing things so ensure that the hardware is not likely to cause injury.

Another category of items that can be used as toys is food. While the basic nutrition can be delivered to the lory in bowls, in the normal man-

Green-naped Lory. Photo by Kristen Bliss

ner, food can also be used to enrich the bird' environment. Many people buy the stainless steel skewers that can hold large pieces of produce and hang from the top of the cage. This gives the bird a toy but also gives him a creative way to feed. Although my lories receive a diced fruit mix, I also give them whole apples or pears, or at least large wedges that are placed loose on the cage bottom. Lories seem to enjoy beating up or rolling around these pieces of fruit and then consuming them. If food items can be delivered in a more natural way the lory will reap the benefits. Wheels of corn on the cob are usually well received, first as a toy and then as an actual source of food. Lories, as well as other parrots, seem to enjoy the process of eating the corn, kernel by kernel. Flowers can be a source of food, so consider leaving the blossom on the branch or stem. Not only will the birds enjoy consuming the flowers, they might enjoy also enjoy the branch and the leaves. Just be sure that branches and flowers are safe. Another way to use food as a toy is to take larger pieces of fruit or vegetables and impale them on safe, natural branches and place them around the cage. Using food as a toy has the benefit of providing both nutrition and entertainment.

Male Or Female

Most lory species are not sexually dimorphic meaning you cannot visually tell the males from the females. If your lory is intended to be a companion bird, knowing its gender is not terribly important. Knowing the sex might help in the naming process if you favor gender specific names;

however, there are not big personality differences between males and females. If you wish to have your bird sexed, there are several methods that can be used. The easiest and least expensive way to determine gender is through DNA. This can be done one of two ways. The first method involves submitting a few freshly pulled feathers. The other involves collecting a tiny amount of blood, usually accomplished by clipping a toenail. There are several laboratories that perform these tests. Upon request, most will send you a free collection kit and instructions. In addition to DNA sexing, gender can be determined by surgical sexing. This is a simple but invasive procedure that must be performed by a veterinarian. The bird is given anesthesia and an endoscope (think fiber optic) is inserted through a tiny incision. Through the scope, the vet can not only look at the internal organs of the bird but also make a determination as to the condition of the reproductive system. This can be especially important for birds that are being set up for breeding. Because of the equipment and expertise required, surgical sexing can sometimes be more expensive than the DNA method. It also involves the use of anesthesia so there are some risks involved with the procedure. If you are uncertain about your vet's ability to surgically sex, be sure to determine how many of the procedures he or she has already performed.

Bathing

Bathing is an essential part of lory keeping. Lories love to bathe and they love getting wet. Bath time is often the highlight of a lory's day and the bird will often approach the event with the same noisy glee it uses to approach life in general. Bathing is a necessary activity that will help keep your bird happy and in good feather condition. You can allow your lory to bathe either by providing a bowl of fresh clean water or by spraying a mist of water directly on it. There are those intrepid souls that will actually take their lory into the shower with them. If you do not provide adequate bathing opportunities you are apt to discover your lory taking matters into its own hands and attempting to bathe in the nectar bowl. I can assure you this will render your bird totally disgusting. I had a pair of yellow streaked lories that always attempted to bathe in their bowl of chopped fruit. Bathing is also playtime so expect it to be noisy and animated. Your bird might need a few moments to calm down afterwards before you try handling it. If there are things you care about in close proximity to the cage, move them. Lories can propel water quite a distance. Stand back and keep towels handy.

Molting

Molting is the process of discarding old feathers and growing new ones. Feathers are like human hair in that they grow in, fall out and grow in again. New feathers, called pinfeathers, grow in to replace the old ones. New feathers are covered in a sheath that, as the feather grows, will dry out and flake off. Lories should molt at least annually although some feather loss will occur throughout the year. If the wing feathers are trimmed to prevent or limit flight, they will eventually be molted out. When the new feathers grow in, your lory will be able to fly again.

Molting can be a stressful time for a bird, especially if it is losing a lot of feathers at once in a heavy molt. Birds can get cranky and short-tempered much in the way teething affects a human baby. When the pinfeathers start coming in, especially around the head where the bird cannot reach, it is nice to assist the process of removing the coverings. Make sure first that there is no blood in the sheath. Then begin gently breaking them apart by rolling them between your fingers, starting at the top and working your way down. If you get too close to a sensitive spot, the bird will let you know. In a flock situation, the lories will preen each other. In captivity, it is your job to perform. When your bird begins looking a bit like a porcupine, it needs your help.

Cleaning And Disinfecting

It is important to keep your bird's cage, bowls, perches, and toys clean and sanitary and it should be part of your lory maintenance routine. There are several components to the cleaning process and none of them are terribly costly or time consuming. By virtue of its diet and droppings, a lory's cage can get sticky quickly. You will need to establish a method for removing dried fruit, nectar and droppings. One of the best ways to manage this is using a garden hose and thoroughly spraying and cleaning the cage. This might not work well in your living room but it is great in the back yard. During nice weather, leave your lory in the cage during the hosing off process and it gets the benefits of a great bath and some fresh air. Use a fiber brush to scrub away dried, caked on debris. Never leave your bird in its cage if you are using any soap, cleaners, or other compounds to clean and disinfect and be sure the surfaces are completely rinsed before allowing your bird to come into contact with them. I suggest you also remove your bird if you plan to use a pressure washer.

In addition to rinsing, there are methods for sanitizing and disinfecting. A disinfectant is an agent that kills germs on surfaces. These germs can cause disease. A sanitizer is something that reduces surface contamination without leaving a residue. One of the cheapest and most commonly available disinfectants is chlorine bleach which kills many types of bacteria and viruses. It becomes inactive in the presence of organic matter so be sure all surfaces are thoroughly rinsed before applying. It can also give off dangerous fumes so it should not be used in direct contact with birds. Never mix bleach with ammonia, as it will create a gas toxic to both humans and birds. When disinfecting with bleach, dilute the solution to one half cup of bleach per gallon of water or one teaspoon to a quart of water. Chlorhexidine is another popular disinfectant, often sold under the brand name Nolvasan®. It is more effective against bacteria than viruses. Another popular disinfecting agent is sold under the name Oxyfresh®. It is made from a chlorine derivative and is relatively effective against many bacteria, viruses, and fungi. When used properly, following the directions, it

can be safe to use around birds. Not all disinfectants are cleaning agents; therefore, be sure the
area is properly cleaned prior to disinfecting. Regardless of the cleaning agent, warm water will
usually increase its effectiveness. Regular soap
does not disinfect but is useful for removing dirt
and built up crud. Some household cleaners can
be effective against both viruses and bacteria; however, they are not without risk. Many can be harmful under direct contact and may not be any more
effective for removing debris than soap and water.
If you do use one of these agents, be sure to rinse
surfaces thoroughly before placing birds back in
the cage.

The dishwasher is a great way to keep bowls
and some perches and toys clean and sanitized.
If the food bowls are heavy plastic or metal they
are probably dishwasher safe. If they are not, consider replacing them with something else.

Disinfecting and sanitizing are not replace-
ments for good husbandry nor should they be
used as your sole means of disease prevention or
elimination. Cleaning and disinfecting is one of
the means you utilize to reduce the occurrence of
disease.

Temperature

Lories housed indoors can withstand whatever
temperature you maintain in your house. If you
can handle it, so can your bird. During the winter they will not suffer should you lower the heat
to 60° F. They can withstand temperatures much
lower than that as long as they are not exposed to

wind. Outside, lories frequently delight in breaking a film of ice on their bath bowl and actually bathing in the frigid water. If your house is 84° F during the summer your lory should not complain. During those warm days be sure not place the cage in the direct sunlight as it streams through the window because it could cause the bird to become overheated. Avoid drafts in the winter and keep the cage away from the heat vents. If you plan to keep your lories outside, they can usually acclimate to the temperature as long as you start them out when the weather is warm. Some species such as the Red-flanked Lorikeet do not adapt well to the colder temperatures so be sure your outdoor lories are hardy enough to cope with your particular winter climate. Lories housed outside should have some sort of shade and cooling during the hot summer months. It is especially important during the colder weather to give your lory a nest box for sleeping. It will also provide shelter from wind and rain as well as a place to get warm. It is always a good idea to check with bird keepers in your area to determine what methods they use to winterize their outdoor flocks.

Lighting

Sunshine is vital to the health of any bird. Birds housed in outdoor cages reap all the benefits of unlimited sunshine but the birds kept inside the home in cages do not. While your bird's cage might be placed in a sunny room, the glass filters out the ultraviolet rays and a bird placed too close to a sunny window may actually become overheated.

Ultraviolet rays, both UVA and UVB, are important for converting Vitamin D into a form that can be utilized. If a bird is unable to convert Vitamin D, health problems can occur including the failure to properly absorb calcium. Providing sufficient ultraviolet rays will improve the health of a bird as well as stimulate the breeding cycle of hens. Additionally, the vision of the bird is vastly improved with correct lighting.

It is possible to provide lighting that includes ultraviolet that is as close as possible to natural sun light. Full spectrum lights provide light balance similar to that of a sunny day at noon without providing additional or unnecessary heat. A scale, known as the Color Rendering Index (CRI), has been developed to compare artificial light with natural sunlight. Natural, unfiltered sunlight reaches a CRI rating of 100, something no artificial light source can achieve. Artificial lighting provided to birds should have a CRI of no less than 90. The lights should be placed as close to the cage as possible but not directly on it. Full spectrum fluorescent lights are available from many sources, from your local hardware store to numerous mail order outlets. They come in an assortment of sizes and prices.

Quarantine

Regardless of where your new bird is obtained, if you have one or more birds already living in your home, quarantining the new bird is a good idea. Many bird owners seem to believe quarantine is an unnecessary precaution if they know the breeder and believe the newly acquired bird to be healthy. The problem with this method of thinking is that sick birds often do not show symptoms of their illness right away so the breeder may be unaware of health problems. In addition, the stress of moving to a new environment may weaken the new bird's immune systems sufficiently to allow it to develop an infection that in turn could be transmitted to other birds. It is not an insult to the reputable breeder or store to quarantine a bird from their facility. In fact it is good management. Proper quarantine procedures involve complete separation of the new bird from any other bird in the home. Because some diseases are transmitted through the air, the ideal quarantine would involve a completely separate air supply. This could be accomplished if you have a separate building in which to house the newcomer or even two totally different air systems in your home. In the absence of a separate air supply, keep the new bird in room by itself, as far away from the other birds as possible. Feed and interact with your new bird after you have taken care of all the others and, unless you are using the dishwasher, wash all its dishes and other items separately from those of your other birds. Before you return to your other birds, be sure to wash your hands thoroughly. Because clothing and shoes can transfer bacteria and disease, remove your shoes before leaving the new bird area. Having a shirt or smock you can throw on over your clothing while you tend to your newest addition will be helpful as long as you remember to remove it before returning to the other parts of your home.

Prior to putting a newly acquired bird into quarantine, check it over carefully, looking for any signs of illness or disease. If there is any question regarding the health of the bird, contact your avian vet immediately.

Well Bird Checkups

A well bird check up is an annual physical examination of the bird, including blood work, which determines the condition and health of your bird. Often it is recommended that newly acquired birds be taken to the vet for a basic check up. This is a personal decision and there is no right or wrong approach. There are several advantages to having at least an initial well bird exam. The blood work can give base line information for such things as uric acid levels. If the bird develops a problem down the road, the initial baseline results give the vet comparison information. Blood work conducted during a well bird check up includes a complete blood count (CBC) and a chemistry panel. Additional testing should also include a fecal gram stain.

A CBC will give an overall picture of the health of the bird. It evaluates both serum and plasma and will measure white and red blood cells, and even some parasites. Results obtained from a CBC can reflect organ disease, nutritional problems, toxins, and certain infections. A chemistry panel tests calcium, protein, uric acid levels, bile acids, glucose, phosphorus, and enzyme activity and gives some idea on the condition and functioning of internal organs. A fecal gram stain tests for abnormal gram-negative bacteria and yeast. Gram-negative bacteria include *E. coli*, Salmonella, Pseudomonas, and Pasteurella. Gram stain is the process of applying dye to a smear on a microscope slide. When the stain is applied to the sample, these bacteria do not stain dark blue or purple. (This has to do with the cell membrane but you will be spared those boring details here.)

Although the best approach to a veterinary examination is to remain in the room with your bird, be sure you are not someone who gets queasy at the sight of blood or needles. Blood is drawn from the jugular vein of the bird and a veterinarian who is experienced with handling birds can perform the draw quickly and with a minimum of stress to the bird. In some cases, such as a large or overly stressed bird, the vet will recommend anesthetizing the bird prior to drawing blood.

Normal Lory Behaviors

Lory behavior can be incredibly entertaining. These birds are non-stop activity and the clowns of the parrot world. They are on the go all the time. While some parrots can be described as "perch potatoes," lories are more like parrots on crack.

Lories have behavior displays that are unique to them and often entertaining to watch. Spend even a small amount of time with one and you'll witness the huffing-hissing routine.

This is when the lory extends and arches its neck in a rather exaggerated fashion, sticks out its tongue and makes a hissing sound. Pet lories are famous for this behavior but even the wild caught birds engage in this display. Head bobbing, while not exclusive to lories, is a very common behavior display. Also seen frequently is their high hopping, running in circles, and fluffed-feather head rubbing. Raising the wings slightly while moving in circles is a display often associated with mating behavior. Your lory may also lower its head, extend the wings slightly and flap. This can be a sign of submission or an attempt to get your attention.

Head bobbing is quite common in lories, especially when they are excited. They will bob repeatedly as if they are keeping time to a tune only they can hear. You will often notice this display in conjunction with your arrival or the arrival of food. Sometimes foot tapping or jumping accompanies the head bobbing. These are symptoms of a happy, well-adjusted lory.

Some parrots have a nice slow walk as they amble in that pigeon-toed manner from one place to another. Not so for lories. If they walk at all it is fast paced and determined. They are on a mission. But for the most part, unlike most other parrots, lories hop. The more the bird acts like a pogo stick, the more excited it is. This is typical of a lory, so full of energy and enthusiasm that it can barely contain itself.

Pinning the eyes is an often-seen behavior that is not unique tolories. This is the contracting of the pupils; usually a warning sign or sign of excitement. Fanning the tail fathers, shrill screeching, and lunging or striking motions with the head may also accompany eye pinning. Attempts to handle a bird displaying these behaviors are often rewarded with aggressive behavior and painful nips.

If you own any type of parrot you can expect to get nipped. Nipping and biting is usually a form of communication. It can also occur when your lory is wound up with excitement and it gets a little carried away. While biting does not normally occur on a regular basis, it does happen occasionally. When it does happen, try not to react loudly or punish the bird.

"Tasting" is a common behavior. While humans rely on their fingers for sensory information, par-

Dusky Lory showing aggressive display

rots use their tongues. When your lory goes exploring with its tongue, don't be surprised or alarmed. It will taste and inspect new objects, foods, and even you the human.

Not to be indelicate but if you think your lory is masturbating, either with your hand or its own toy or perch, it probably is. While not our favorite lory behavior it is not uncommon or abnormal regardless of gender.

Under the category of Not-So-Normal-Behavior is sleeping on the cage bottom. While most lories prefer a nest box, hammock, or other shelter for roosting, there is the occasional lory that defies the stereotype. If your lory is one of these oddballs, the first time you witness this peculiar habit you will be quite startled, for anything lying motionless on the cage floor tends to be a bad sign. And if your lory is a particularly sound sleeper, those heart-stopping moments will last longer than you would like. I had one lory, a wild caught Red, who often slept in this manner. And because she was a deep sleeper, she did not always respond when I approached the cage. I never got used to finding her lying seemingly lifeless on the floor of the cage with her little feet in the air and I experienced regular moments of horror for years.

The "Terrible Twos" is a common although not enjoyable behavior. This is the phase your lory goes through as it makes the transition from adorable little baby into a more mature bird. You will know your bird has entered this phase when one day it seems as if your sweet and lovable lory has disappeared, only to be replaced by its evil twin Skippy. Your normally mild mannered bird is out of control with playing and all other activity. Previously gentle, your lory begins delivering painful bites for no apparent reason. This period usually does not last more than a couple of weeks. You will know your bird has passed the phase when Skippy has departed as suddenly as he arrived and your wonderful bird has returned. In mature birds this type of behavior may appear periodically as it experiences the hormonal surges associated with the breeding season.

Feather Maintenance

Maintaining their plumage is important for birds and so they devote quite a bit of time to preening and feather care. One of the strangest grooming behaviors exhibited by our feathered friends, although not unique to lories, is called anting. Ants secrete formic acid, and in a natural setting, birds use the ants to deliver this substance to their feathers. Most likely, formic acid, while annoying to humans, does not bother birds and may actually kill annoying little mites and other pesky things. When real ants are not available, lories will use whatever is handy, favoring orange peels, eucalyptus leaves, and even broccoli. They will actively ant, taking whatever item they have and applying it to or tucking it into their feathers, paying special attention to their wings.

Another plumage maintenance behavior is preening. All parrots preen their feathers in order to remove the sheaths and bits of debris and to restore them to their pristine nature. Preening goes on every day so do not be alarmed if you see your bird engaging in this behavior. Preening is not the same as feather destruction although at times they look similar. Lories also have a preening mode that can only be described as power preening or speed preening. They run their beaks rapidly through their feathers in a manner that seems to do little more than reflect the hyper state that is natural for a lory.

Because they are active, playful creatures, lory tail feathers can become quite tattered or broken. This is normal and not usually a sign of a problem. Climbing up and down the sides of the cage along with active playing causes the majority of the tail feather mess. Some lories manage to maintain their tail feathers in good condition; others destroy them as soon as they grow in. Sometime the direction of the cage bars can make a difference; however, you might just have to learn to live with your bird's imperfect tail feathers.

Talking

Birds do not have vocal chords or lips so they are not using the same equipment to speak that humans use. They utilize an organ that is similar but not identical to the human larynx. This organ, called the syrinx, is part of the trachea. Sounds are produced in the syrinx by the flow of air past the membranes within the organ and controlled by the bronchial muscles

Parrots learn to speak and mimic by association. You may notice them imitating household
and environmental sounds. Included in these
sounds is the sound of human speech, either in
individual words or whole phrases and sentences.
And, the more consistent the sound, the more
likely your bird will be to learn and use it. Lories
can also learn by association so if you greet them
every morning with a cheerful "good morning" you
might find that ultimately, they greet you the same
way at the appropriate time. The exceptions to
learning by repetition are things that are said with
great excitement and emotion. For example you
may say "pretty bird' to the lory every day with no
results but the first time you drop the bowl of
green beans on your way to the dinner table and
utter an expletive, be aware that your bird might
repeat that having heard it only once. Some sounds
are harder than others to mimic. Birds do not
have lips but they still manage to mimic some of
the more difficult sounds such as the letter "B."
Keep in mind that not every parrot will learn to
speak and lories are no exception. While lories
are not reputed to be the parrot world's most capable talkers and mimics, you will find that some
of them do quite well. For the most part their enun-
ciation is not terribly clear compared to other parrots and their voices often sound like parodies of
our own. For those who wish to have a more tal-
ented talker, African Greys, Amazons, and even
Mynahs are more capable. But we all know it is
not the talking ability that draws us to lories.

Anthropomorphism And Behavior

Anthropomorphizing is the practice of assigning human traits or personality to something that

Duyvenbode's Lory. Photo by Richard Brncato

is not human. Parrots are very intelligent creatures and it has often been speculated that many of them operate on the level of a human toddler. They often speak to us in our own language so it's easy to forget they are both birds and wild animals and instead think of them as our children. Falling into the habit of thinking of your lory as your child or a feathered kid can be doing both of you grave disservice. It is not a child; it is a wild bird. It thinks like a bird and acts like a bird. It does not understand the world around it in terms of human thought and emotions. Much of the behavior you see in your bird is essentially programmed into it. The things it fears or likes are mostly instinctive. Parrots do not think, process, act, and react like humans. So, it is up to the human to attempt to understand and interpret the actions of the bird.

Lories are highly social flock creatures. When you remove the bird from its normal existence in the wild, you the human, become part of the flock. Your lory will make noises that seem constant and annoying to you. To the lory, they are contact calls. You are out of its range of vision so it must make contact with you and determine your location. It is helpful to respond to your bird when it calls to you. Your bird will generally not need contact calls when it is in the same room with you. In addition to the periodic contact calls, there are two periods during the day that lories seem to have the occasion for making noise. In the morning there is a call to the flock, telling everyone to come feed. In the evening there is the flock call to come home to roost. These calls may seem a little noisy and unnecessary to you but in a wild habitat they would broadcast to the flock the location of the food or the roosting spot. If you have other birds in your home, they will respond to these flock calls, resulting in what seems to be a jungle-like cacophony. These louder than normal calls can go on for a period of time, five to fifteen minutes seems to be the norm. Loud is good in the forested expanse of New Guinea where the flock's range might be many miles. Lories do not understand about using an indoor voice. Unfortunately, lories do not have the sweet, beautiful voices of songbirds and their calls can be quite shrill. There is little you can to do train these behaviors out of your bird. Fortunately most lories are not given to frequent bouts of prolonged or intense calling and most lory owners become used to, possibly even amused by, the sound. What is a grating noise to one person's ears is music to another's.

Biting is another behavior that makes no sense to humans. Often it seems vicious and unwarranted. There are several reasons humans get bitten by their birds but it is not out of meanness or spite. One big reason is that humans fail to read their bird and its body language. Lories are good at showing just what kind of mood they are in. If they are wound up with their playing, and especially if they are busy "killing" a toy, you can bet that isn't a good time to ask it to step up and return to its cage. There is a high probability you will get bitten. It takes a little time for a lory to wind down from its excitement. In this way perhaps they are a bit like small children. Warning bites are another misinterpreted behavior. You are peacefully hanging out with your lory and for no apparent reason it leans over and nips at you. Often this happens when someone enters the room but there can be other changes in the environment that might provoke this as well. In the wild when there is a perceived threat or change, the bird would nip at its mate or another bird, forcing it to fly away from the danger. What's happening is your bird is actually taking care of you by warning you to escape. Biting can also occur at other times. Sexually mature birds can become hormonal and this can cause some changes in behavior that might include the occasional nip. Molting can also be a difficult and somewhat uncomfortable, stressful time for your bird. A little grumpier than normal, you might find your lory has become momentarily less tolerant of your intrusions. Another popular cause of biting is when your lory becomes protective of its cage. Having you suddenly reach in its cage for no reason the bird can understand might provoke biting.

While humans may never completely understand the behaviors of these wonderful birds, it helps to get to know the bird and its behaviors. Body language worth noting includes fluffing up its body with the tail feathers spread wide, pinning the eyes (the pupils contract and expand), and lunging. These are all warning behaviors. Failure to heed the warning can result in the need for band-aids. Your bird should never be scolded or punished for biting because it is only trying to communicate the best way it can. Remember, it is just being a bird.

The Internet

Once you've discovered the wonderful world of lories you will be anxious to learn more. Not too many years ago it was next to impossible to find information about lories. Occasionally a publication would run an article about some aspect of lories but the information was limited in scope and rarely directed one to additional sources.

Today, the largest source of readily available and free information is the Internet. While the 'Net seems rife with information one must approach it cautiously. Birdkeeping is not an exact science. There are no specific guidelines that will carry a lory lover safely through the life of the bird. The Internet, while certainly a source of useful information, is an anonymous forum where anyone can be anything, including an expert. Use caution when utilizing the Internet and keep an open mind. Not only is it a great source of good information it is also a great source of misinformation. Everyone with a keyboard, mouse and modem has a thought or opinion on how the rest of us should keep our birds and broadcasts said thoughts and opinions at regular intervals.

When separating the wheat from the chaff, try to become familiar with your sources. Always remember that just because it appears on a web site does not make it the most relevant or accurate information. Signing on to an e-mail list for lories can be quite helpful but get a feel for the

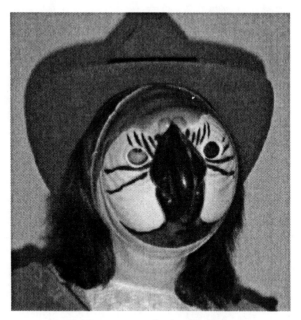

*The Internet can be anonymous. Do you
have any idea with whom you're dealing?*

people giving the advice and suggestions. Ask yourself some questions before blindly following the directions of strangers. Do they in fact have experience with lories and if so, how much? Do others in the online community know them, respect their input, and solicit recommendations from them? Do they get angry or abusive when you or others question their information or disagree with their advice? Must they always have the last word? Do they seem generous with their expertise, taking the time to thoroughly answer questions and even follow up? The answers to these questions might help you determine which anonymous entities are most likely giving the soundest advice. Remember that the Internet can be impersonal and anonymous. Everyone can pretend to be an expert and you do not always know whom you are talking to.

Even when you have found one or more sources for what you consider to be reliable information, keep in mind that there are as many ways to keep these birds as there are people keeping them. While one person may have great success with their routine and protocols, you may not do as well. Look at all the available information, perhaps even combine a number of good points, and find the methods that work for you and your birds.

Lories In Zoos

At one time, lories were relatively uncommon in homes and aviaries and the best place to encounter them was at a zoo or similar facility. While previously displayed in cages like all the other birds, zoos have now found that the interactive aviaries allow people to see more of these birds' beauty and personality. The opportunity to spend a little bit of money on a tiny cup of nectar to feed to one of these lories is great fun and delights children and adults of all ages. The popularity of walk-through zoo exhibits has increased the visibility of lories, and subsequently, their popularity. One of the down sides to the boon in interactive aviaries is that the acquisition process may cause periods where some types of lories are not available for sale to the general public because the zoos are buying them up, dozens at a time. Interactive lory exhibits have become so widespread that there may be one in a zoo near you.

Check with your local zoo, keeping in mind these aviaries might be seasonal. While these exhibits are not an inexpensive addition to a zoo's exhibits, they are quite popular with the visitors. An interactive aviary filled with assorted lory species that come right down and land on you to drink cups of nectar is often as up close and personal as some people can get to birds. And having a beautiful little bird alight on your head or arm is pretty up close and personal! Being able to spend a few minutes with such brilliantly colored creatures can awaken a visitor's interest and appreciation for the mysterious and beautiful members of the parrot family. Visitors to these exhibits should be cautious around the birds and understand that while they have no fear of alighting on a human, they are not necessarily tame enough to pet and play with. Painful nips can be the result of attempting this. Another caution when entering a walk- through lory exhibit is that the birds have often figured out how undo buttons. Check your clothing before departing the exhibit.

Lories do not always do well in colony situations; however, if the birds are young enough and the species compatible, it can be accomplished. The birds in the colony should be youngsters and when they approach breeding age should be removed. Once a colony has been established, care should be exercised when adding a new lory. Although the rainbow lories seem to be the most popular birds for this type of exhibit some *Eos* species (i.e. Red, Blue-streaked, and Violet-naped Lories) will also work. Apparantly the *Chalcopsitta* species are less suited to this type of environment and their aggressive nature can be dangerous to the other occupants. I have a pair of Yellow-streaked lories that had to be removed from an exhibit because their aggression was endangering other birds in the aviary. Black-capped and Chattering Lories can also be difficult in a colony situation. Goldie's Lorikeets on the other hand can do well in a colony situation. While they may not be the best birds for a zoo exhibit they can be delightful additions to a mixed species aviary.

Traveling With Your Lory

Green-naped Lories at Busch Gardens, Tampa FL
Photo by John Culver

Having a bird doesn't need to tie you down. If you are ready to hit the road and you are not sure what to do about your lory, you have several options. You can leave the bird behind with a reliable sitter, either in your home or somewhere else. Pet stores and veterinarians will often board a bird for a small daily fee. Or, you can take it with you. Traveling with a bird on an airplane is fairly simple and straightforward. First, you must determine if the airline you intend to use allows live animals as either cargo or carry-on and what costs are involved. You might be required to provide a health certificate from a veterinarian. If the bird is going to be carried on to the aircraft, there is usually a charge for doing so plus a reservation must be made in advance. The carrier you use must be small enough to fit under the seat in front of you. If your bird is going to be shipped as cargo, it should be placed in a crate or container that is approved for airline shipping. It must be ventilated and it must be shaped in a manner so that air can get to it when items are stacked directly up against it. These crates can be purchased at most pet stores and the labels should indicate if they are airline approved. Check with the airline well in advance of your scheduled to trip to determine if there are any special requirements or regulations.

If you choose to take your lory on a road trip in the car with you, the preparations need not be elaborate. You will need some basic items such as a temporary cage, preferably collapsible, to house the bird at the final destination; some sort of carrier or cage for the bird to actually travel in; blankets for both warmth and darkness; a good supply of all the necessary food items; some bottled water in case the local supply tastes funny to your bird; a favorite toy or two; and finally, a small airline type pet carrier. While you might have a cage that can be fastened in with a seat belt, a small pet carrier is essential should you break down and need to depart the scene in a tow truck or police car. If it is cold, the blanket can be thrown over the carrier or cage in the car and while being transported your bird will stay warmer. It will also provide cover for the bird should you need to stop at a rest stop or move the cage while the bird is sleeping. If the trip is particularly long, using a softer perch like the ones made from firm rope might be more comfortable on the bird's feet than hard wood or concrete.

While it might seem kinder to allow your bird to be out of its cage while riding in the car, it is not safe for either of you. If you have to hit the brakes suddenly, the bird might become a projectile. It could easily be injured or killed, even in a minor fender bender or when cut off in traffic. In the event of an accident or breakdown, an uncontained bird can easily escape if the doors are opened suddenly or the window is lowered or broken. A loose bird can become upset or frightened which in turn can startle the driver. A driver who does not have full attention focused on the road can be a hazard on any highway. A loose bird can meander about the car and find itself in interesting places such as near the gas or brake pedals. For the safety of both the bird and the occupants of the vehicle, keep the bird in a cage that in turn is fastened in place.

Chapter 3
BREEDING LORIES

Suddenly you find yourself with two opposite sex birds of the same species and you are thinking perhaps you could become a breeder. These adult birds are great and young chicks would be even more fun. Put your head between your knees until that feeling goes away. In the event the feeling does not go away, there are some things to consider before hanging up the nest box.

Do you have a market for the birds you intend to raise? Sure, it seems like everyone is snatching up those beautiful lories like you have right now but to whom will you be selling and what means will you use to unite bird and new owner? Many bird breeders use the airlines to ship birds around; however, this is not particularly cheap or convenient. If you live in a more rural area, airline shipping might not be an easy option so the presence of a local market must be explored.

If you think you have the market nailed down, are you willing to commit the time, energy, and expense to raising birds? Hand rearing birds is a huge commitment of time and resources. You must devote around the clock attention to the birds because they require food at regular intervals. Clutches of birds can hatch at the most inopportune times, like right before you are going on vacation. Will you be able to take the babies with you, keep them warm, and feed them regularly? If not, do you have a reliable caretaker and feeder? Will that person be able to care for the chicks in your absence if there is a problem? You must also be ready to devote anywhere from seven to sixteen weeks to rearing the chicks. If the parent birds do not feed the newly hatched baby, you will have to take it, place it in the brooder, and feed it every hour or two around the clock. This can get old really fast so if you're not inclined to give up sleep and your normal activities, reconsider the breeding thing. Even if the parents do feed the chick, you will most likely want to pull it at about fourteen days of age and hand feed it. This tames them and allows them to become good pets. At two weeks, most chicks will require feeding every three to four hours, with an eight to twelve hour break that allows the crop to completely empty. If you have a full time job you will need to do one of two things. You must to be free to take the bird to work and feed it there. If not, you can use the time you are at work as the period when the crop empties completely but be willing to give up your sleep in exchange for feeding it every couple of hours through the night.

Breeding birds is not cheap. The cost of the birds themselves might lead you into thinking that you can make a bunch of money raising birds. Think again. You will need to make an initial investment in equipment and supplies. You will need the appropriate cage and nest box. Once the chicks arrive you will need a brooder, substrate, leg bands, hand feeding formula, syringes or other means of delivering food to chicks, a gram scale, a weaning cage, a carrier, and a host of other things not mentioned here. Because successful breeding is not a guarantee, you must still manage the costs of maintaining the pair until such time as they do produce offspring. That could be several years, if ever, with no means to offset the expense through the sale of chicks.

When paired with their own kind, birds will often cease being lovable pets and become bonded to each other. When making the decision to pair birds you must be willing to give up the companion relationship you have with them. There are some instances where former pets remain sweet and manageable to humans while successfully mating and rearing chicks but you cannot assume that is what will happen in your case.

Compatible pairing and fertile egg production are not guaranteed when setting up pairs of lories for breeding. The very first thing to beware of is birds sold as pairs and, worse yet, "proven pairs." Many seasoned breeders have found themselves in possession of a "pair" of birds that turns out to be two birds, both the same species and gender. Be sure your birds are correctly sexed before pairing them. Once you determine you have one of each gender there are still no guarantees of successful breeding. There are those occasions when two birds of the same species might not like each other so it is important to monitor the behavior when birds are placed together in a cage. Introduce them to each other gradually by placing them in separate cages side by side. This allows them to see each other and get used to each other's presence. If they seem to be interested in one another and perhaps are perching as close as possible in their separate quarters, place them in a neutral cage. Putting a lory into a cage already occupied by another lory might cause territorial behavior and aggression. If the birds are not compatible, separate them immediately before injuries occur.

Just because the birds bond instead of assaulting each other, do not assume fertile lory eggs will be in your future. There are many variables that determine breeding success. They range from adequate housing and diet to proper humidity and incubation. Some lories that were originally tame, hand fed pets make poor breeders. This is not always the case so do not assume your pet will not be suited to breeding. Not every pair of lories will produce fertile eggs let alone incubate and feed. Some birds, while very bonded, are unable or unwilling to breed. Perhaps the reproductive system of one does not work properly. Causes of that could be anything from congenital problems to age. Some lories are just too busy playing and being lories to get down to the serious business of reproduction. Not every hen immediately figures out the part where she's supposed to sit on those eggs for a couple weeks. For that matter it may take an egg or two before she gets the idea to lay them in the nest box rather than off a perch. There are those lories, usually males, who will destroy the eggs either shortly after they have been laid or as the chicks are pipping or hatching. This is often the result of boredom. Offering elements of a natural environment, such as branches and flowers and placing food containers in several different locations, may help with both the tedium of life in a cage and the lack of exercise.

When setting up a pair of lories for breeding, the caging requirements will be quite different than what you would use for a pet. To begin with, these birds will need a space large enough to accommodate both of them, allowing for plenty or room to move, perch, exercise, and even fly (breeder birds should be flighted). For even the smallest lories, the cage should be a minimum of four feet deep and three feet tall. This will not fit nicely in your living room. And even if it did, you probably want to avoid having nesting birds in an area that has heavy traffic, noise, and activity. In addition to a sufficiently large cage, you will need a nest box. The size and shape would depend on the species being bred. A square cockatiel size nest box works well with small lories such as Iris, Scaly-breasted and Goldie's. A boot or "L" shaped boxes work well for many of the larger lory species. The nest box is attached to the side of the cage and the opening should be large enough to allow them to enter and exit freely. While lories are not as inclined to chew and destroy as other parrots, they will modify the opening to some degree. Once the nest box is hung, it will need to be filled with a clean, dry substrate. Pine or aspen shavings are inexpensive and available in most pet stores. Never use cedar shavings. Other substances can be used, but when selecting them, be sure they are not something that can cause a problem such as crop impaction when ingested by chicks.

After all this, if you're still ready to attempt lory breeding, there is more you might need to know. Lories usually lay a clutch of one or two eggs although on occasion they might lay three eggs. For almost all species, incubation begins when the first egg is laid and is normally carried out by the hen. The incubation period varies depending on the species. Average incubation period for Rainbow Lories is twenty two to twenty four days; for Red Lories it is twenty four or so days; Black-capped and Purple-naped Lories might go as long as twenty seven days. Goldie's average about twenty three days. Lory chicks hatch with their eyes closed. At the age of approximately ten to fourteen days, the eyes begin to open.

While the hen is on eggs and, more importantly, after the eggs hatch, the amount of food given to the pair should be increased. Lory chicks hatch with their eyes closed and most are covered with white down. The down gives way to pin feathers and the eyes will begin to open at about ten days of age. When the eyes begin to open, the birds can be removed from the nest box and placed in a warm brooder. Prior to removing the chicks, they should be banded. The information placed on the band is a matter of personal preference. It usually includes the state of residence, year of hatch, and a number. The band size will vary depending on the type of lory involved.

Because young lory chicks do not have feathers to keep them warm, the brooder temperature should be kept in the range of 94° F to 97° F depending on the down covering them. As the down becomes heavy and the feathers develop, the temperature can slowly be lowered into the '80s. If the chick appears to be panting, it is too hot and the brooder temperature should be lowered. If the chicks are bunched up together and seem lethargic, they are probably too cold. If there is only one chick in the brooder, the temperatures will be a little bit higher than it would be for two or more. Once the birds have feathered out on their heads, breasts, and wings, they can be kept at room temperature. If the ambient temperature is below 75° F they may need to remain in a heated brooder until they have sufficient feathering to remain warm and comfortable at lower temperatures.

If you have not had the experience of hand-feeding a bird yourself you would be wise to seek the help of a more experienced breeder. While lories are not particularly difficult to feed, there are some problems that may occur if you are not familiar with the process. The best way to deliver formula or nectar to a young chick is through a syringe. Now these are not syringes that actually have needles attached. These are syringes with open tips. Some breeders use those little paper cups you use at water coolers or in bathrooms. You can put the nectar in that and kind of pinch the sides together in a "V" and tip it to the bird's beak. I am not terribly fond of this method primarily because I like to measure exactly how much the bird receives at each feeding. Also, depending on the feeding response I get from a particular chick, I do not enjoy wiping formula off the

Lories enjoy their privacy.

walls and ceiling. If you decide to use syringes, start with a supply of those that hold ten cc's. These are the right size for most lories. Syringes should always be cleaned and disinfected after each use. Formula or nectar should never be saved and reheated and the container you mix it in should be cleaned and disinfected each time.

Prior to embarking on the handfeeding adventure you will need a good digital thermometer. Whether using handfeeding formula or lory nectar, it must be heated to about 105° F. If it is cold it may not pass through the crop properly or the chick might refuse to eat it. If it is too hot, it can burn the crop causing problems for the chick. The best method of mixing formula is to heat the water and mix it with the dry formula. If the formula is mixed up and then heated in the microwave, there is a serious risk of "hot spots" which can cause burns in the crop. To keep the formula warm while you're feeding, fill a bowl (preferably glass or china) with heated water in which you can set the cup containing formula. It is also good to have a mentor locally; someone who has experience in hand rearing and with some of the problems one might encounter. This is especially important when attempting to feed chicks from day one. If you have no previous hand feeding experience you run the risk of aspiration, crop burns, even malnutrition without someone available to teach you this technique. There is a myth that persists in aviculture that if one feeds and weans out their pet bird, they will develop a stronger bond. This is not true. A good breeder will raise tame and socialized birds that will adapt to any loving home. The bond you develop with a bird this way will not be any weaker for not having weaned the bird yourself.

There are several accepted methods for hand rearing lory chicks. Most breeders will use a commercial handfeeding formula, commercial lory nectar, or a combination of both. I personally start them on formula and switch them to nectar and pureed fruit because that is what they would be eating if their parents were feeding them. A newly hatched day-one chick should not start right out with food. These birds should get a small amount of electrolyte solution before they receive any food. When chicks are first pulled at the standard ten to fourteen days, start them out on handfeeding formula and mix it according to the directions. After a day or so, I begin adding the powdered nectar mix to the formula. I gradually increase the amount of nectar while decreasing the amount of formula until I am feeding nectar only. I make the nectar a bit thicker than I do for my adult lories. If the birds are eating well and gaining weight, I add pureed fruit or organic baby food/ fruit to the nectar.

Every day, when the crop is empty before the first feeding, weigh the chicks and record the weights. This is an important tool for monitoring health and progress. Weight gain varies depending on the species and other factors such as formula and temperature.

Scaly-breasted Lories

Once the chicks are feathering out nicely and beginning to explore their environment, you can begin introducing solid food. Place a dish of diced fruit or soft veggies and a small bowl of nectar on the floor of the cage and allow the youngsters to explore. This is also the time to introduce toys and perches. Because young birds are naturally curious, they will check out the food and toys. In the beginning it may seem they are playing with the food more than they are actually eating it and this is a normal part of the exploration process. Place a perch close to the bottom of the cage and they will figure out what to do quickly. Ultimately the chicks will depend more on food they find for themselves and less on you. The weaning time for chicks will depend on the species and the hand feeder. Most lories wean easily but never count on that to happen with the clutch you are raising.

While raising lories can be a rewarding experience, it is a responsibility that should not be taken lightly and a commitment that should not be entered impulsively.

Chapter 4
LORIES IN
HEALTH AND SICKNESS

A happy, healthy lory is one who is energetic, alert and active, and who vocalizes frequently and loudly. It has a hearty appetite, rarely stops playing until the lights go out, and sometimes seems totally out of control; much in the same way a toddler might behave. Its eyes and nares are clear and the feathers glossy. With a good diet, plenty of fresh water and exercise, your lory should be your companion for many years. The life expectancy of pet lories seems to be similar to that of a cat or dog.

Lories are parrots and, like all parrots, are still wild animals. Even though your bird was hatched in captivity it is only a generation or two removed from the wild. As wild animals, they utilize many wild behaviors that we humans do not understand. They are prey animals. This very fact makes it difficult for us to detect health problems. Parrots will mask any symptoms of illness until it is usually too late. In the wild, showing signs of sickness or weakness would make them especially vulnerable to predators. With a companion bird this makes it especially difficult to detect any signs of stress or illness.

One of the most important elements to owning any exotic bird is having a competent avian vet whom you trust. Once you have a good vet lined up, it is very important for the sake of your bird to develop a good working relationship with him or her. Before you bring the first bird into your home, you should have lined up a veterinarian who has experience working with birds. It's also a good idea to have a back up avian vet, just in case. You might have need for a second opinion or you may not be able to get an immediate appointment with one. Additionally, you should know where to take your bird in case of an emergency, as they never seem to happen during normal business hours. Some veterinarians see emergencies on evenings and weekends but in some cases you might have to take your bird to an emergency clinic. There are many ways to locate a vet who is right for you and your bird. The American Board of Veterinary Practitioners (ABVP) has an avian certification with some fairly rigorous requirements. Once completing the requirements and sitting the exam, a vet can become "Board Certified" in avian practice. Because the certification process is not only rigorous but also time consuming, taking several years to complete, there are not a large number of Board Certified avian vets available. While Board Certification indicates the vet possesses experience and a body of knowledge, there is no assurance that you will like or get along with the vet. It is also not necessarily an indication of the veterinarian's skill or dedication to the practice of avian medicine. You can determine if there is one in your area by conducting a search of the ABVP web site at www.abvp.com. There is also an organization known as the Association of Avian Veterinarians (AAV). This is a professional organization of vets who have an interest in avian medicine. Membership in the organization does not equal extensive knowledge or experience but it does give an idea of vets in the area that might be able to care for your bird. You can locate a member of the AAV in your area by searching their web site at www.aav.org. One of the best ways to locate an avian vet however is by word of mouth and referral. If you obtained your bird from a local breeder, find out their choice for veterinary care. If there is a local bird club, its members might have recommendations. Finding a vet whose clients feel confident is often a good place to start with the care of your own bird.

While it is essential to have veterinary care available, the first line of defense for the health of your bird is you, the owner. You are the one who sees and interacts with your bird daily. You are the one who will notice subtle changes in it. A careful daily examination of your bird physically (eyes, nares, keel bone, feather condition), its behavior and demeanor, food intake or lack of, and droppings can sometimes help identify illness. Less energy, talking and chirping less, perching with unusual posture, and experiencing a rapid weight loss can all be signs that it is in distress. The keel bone is the long bone that runs vertically down your bird's breast. If this bone becomes sharp or prominent, that is an indication of weight loss. Weighing your bird on a gram scale in the circumstances can be useful. Your bird will often sit quietly with its feathers fluffed out in an effort to keep itself warm. Disease can alter the droppings. Lory droppings are runny to begin with but look for any changes in color or consistency. When doing this, keep in mind things the bird has consumed in the last twenty four hours. High concentrations of things like carrot juice or dark berries, or the dyes in colored food pellets can change the color of the droppings on even the healthiest bird. Seeing the change for the first time can be rather unsettling but it is natural. If the bird has not had anything different or unusual in its diet and the droppings have changed, your bird might be falling ill. If its feathers are fluffed, the bird is having trouble staying warm. At that point you can fashion a brooder/incubator using common household items. An aquarium or small plastic tub will serve as the container. A heating pad under half of the container, covered with towels to prevent burning, can keep the bird warm. Cover the container with a towel, monitor the temperature to ensure it does not rise too high, and isolate the bird. It should be kept calm and dark until you are able to get treatment. It is important to contact an avian vet at the very first sign of trouble. If the veterinarian prescribes medication for your bird it is critically important to be sure you completely understand the instructions and give the correct dosage.

Lories are susceptible to the same diseases and ailments common in companion birds. They are susceptible to bacterial and fungal infections. Because their droppings are so moist it is important to keep the cage substrate clean and dry to inhibit the growth of mold and limit the possibility of aspergillosis. Beak and Feather disease (PBFD) plagued lory populations in the United States during the 1990s. Lories can get Proventricular Dilatation Disease (PDD). If you suspect your lory suffers from this ailment, contact your avian vet immediately. Lories can also succumb to fatty liver disease. Visceral gout in lories is not uncommon. In addition to the common ailments, lories appear to be a group that has become vulnerable to hemochromatosis, also known as iron storage disease.

Liver problems are not uncommon in caged birds and lories are no exception. The liver acts as a filter, removing toxins from the body. As such, it becomes exposed to myriad toxins. The liver is unique in that it can regenerate a portion of itself after an insult; however, these toxins, over a period of time, will begin to do damage to the liver.

Less is known about the health issues of lories than other psittacines, making it even more important for owners to have a complete necropsy performed when one dies.

Common Disorders Found In Lories

Fatty Liver Disease

In psittacines, fatty liver, or hepatic lipidosis, has become an all too common affliction affecting many lories as well as other parrots. It is exactly what it sounds like – a high concentration of fat built up in the liver. The liver can continue to function with a significant degree of damage and the bird will show no signs of disease. As the fat accumulates, liver function becomes compromised and the potential for long-term damage increases. It is widely believed that this ailment is caused by a diet high in fat, combined with the relative inactivity and lack of exercise common to caged birds. Many birds are fed a diet high in fat, which can predispose them to developing fatty liver disease. While lipids are the primary source of energy, when birds do not have the natural ability to burn it up, problems can occur.

Although lories usually do not eat a diet that includes the high fat, dried seeds that other parrots receive, they are still at risk. The most effective way to prevent this ailment is to allow your lory to get plenty of exercise, feed it a balanced diet, low in fat and carbohydrates, and as free as possible from toxins that can insult the liver. Sources of toxins that can potentially damage the liver include medications, stress, dietary imbalance, chemicals occurring in the food and water supply, airborne toxins such as smoke and pollution and mold. Foods that are good for a healthy liver include fresh fruits and vegetables such as dark leafy greens, red peppers, squash, berries and apples, and sprouted seeds.

While Fatty Liver disease tends to be asymptomatic, there are some signs that might indicate a potential problem, including obesity, abdominal distention, dyspnea (difficulty breathing), overgrown beak and toenails, poor feather condition, and lethargy. While some of these signs may be present, a diagnosis can only be made through blood testing and radiographs (x-rays).

Treatment for this problem is more supportive than curative. There are allopathic or conventional medical treatments including the use of the drug Lactulose, which eases the burden on the liver, and the addition of certain vitamins to assist the liver in metabolizing fat. Antibiotics are also sometimes prescribed, especially in the case of secondary infections, but they can actually place undue stress on the liver. There are also homeopathic treatments that include detoxifying and the use of herbs such as milk thistle.

Hemochromatosis (Iron Storaqe Disease)

Hemochromatosis, also known as Iron Storage Disease, is a metabolic disorder that causes an unusually large amount of iron to be accumulated in body tissue. In lories it is potentially lethal. While much is known about this disorder in humans, one should be cautioned against drawing too many parallels with its effects in birds. In avian species the causes are unknown but veterinarians and aviculturists believe it to be a combination of several factors including diet, evolution, and genetics. This disease has been most commonly associated with soft billed birds such as mynahs, toucans, and birds of paradise but there is growing evidence to indicate that lories may also be a species vulnerable to this disorder

There have not been many studies conducted on avian hemochromatosis; therefore, much of what is commonly believed about the disorder is speculation. Most of the information relating to Iron Storage Disease and lories is anecdotal and as such is not always appropriate data for an actual scientific discussion.

In most cases, hemochromatosis is asymptomatic until shortly before death. When evident, symptoms can include difficulty breathing, fluid in the air sacs, paralysis, and distended abdomen. Actual diagnosis is most commonly made during a necropsy. In living birds, tests conducted on tissue retrieved from a liver biopsy can make a specific diagnosis. Radiographs and blood work on live birds can indicate liver disorders that may include iron storage but will not accurately diagnose the disorder itself. Other tests often are not particularly helpful in determining status of hemochromatosis in a living bird. If diagnosed in a living bird, there are some treatments available, although some of the results are questionable. Phlebotomy, drawing blood equal to 1% of the bird's body weight on a regular basis, is acceptable treatment. It is not always a practical one, especially on aviary birds not used to being handled. Chelation is another possible treatment. Some human drugs have been used experimentally on birds with limited success.

The more available the iron is the more readily it can be extracted and stored in the tissue. Diets that contain animal protein sources can be higher in available dietary iron than those using plant protein sources. Another factor that assists the absorption of iron is ascorbic acid, commonly found in citrus fruits. The acid can release the tightly bound iron from plants and make it more available. While many aviculturists have used citrus successfully, the use of it is something to consider when developing your total diet.

While diet can play a role in the development of hemochromatosis, it can also occur when there are relatively low levels of dietary iron. Genetics must also be considered a factor. In some regions, dietary iron may be practically nonexistent, and birds must adapt by becoming better able to process and store necessary iron. It is possible that lories have evolved into one of the groups that process iron too efficiently thereby absorbing and storing all available iron. Kept in captivity, these birds are fed a diet that, even while it is considered to be low in iron, has a much higher iron content than that which would be found in their wild habitats. It also appears that birds who are prone to iron storage do not decrease the uptake of iron when the amount stored is adequate. Because of the limited bloodlines available in captive lories, we may be breeding certain predispositions into them.

When this disorder shows up, it is in lories around five or six years of age; however, it has been discovered in birds much younger than that who have been fed a diet extremely high in iron content. It is ultimately a fatal disorder that can take months, even years, to develop and become severe enough to result in death. The prevalence of hemochromatosis in lories is not well documented; therefore, it is not known if it has become a common problem in our captive population.

There are some preventive measures that can be taken to keep lories from acquiring this disorder including feeding a well balanced diet that is low in iron. A diet that contains less than 100 parts per million (ppm) of iron is considered to be low in iron. Periodic testing of commercial lory diets has revealed that the iron content in all of them fall below that level.

Visceral Gout

Of the many health concerns plaguing caged birds, one that seems to appear often enough to cause some concern is gout, which is brought on by the build up of uric acid. Uric acid is produced by the liver and excreted through the kidneys. It is the result of metabolizing nitrogen that is present in the food. The uric acid itself is not toxic or harmful but the build up of crystals can severely damage body tissue. The build-up of uric acid crystals is the result of the inability of the kidneys to remove from the blood the waste products resulting from nitrogen metabolism. The uric acid, when not properly removed from the blood stream, will begin to crystallize and collect in various places in the bird's body. Accumulation in the joints and surrounding tissues, usually in the legs and feet, is articular gout. This is considered to be the chronic form of gout and it presents as swelling in the joints and can cause the inability to properly balance and perch or lameness. Visceral Gout is build up of uric acid crystals in the various internal organs (viscera) and it is considered the acute form of the disease.

The exact cause of visceral gout is not clear but it appears there are a variety of factors that might cause a predisposition. It is often associated with high levels of dietary protein and calcium, Vitamin D3 hypervitaminosis, insufficient levels of Vitamin A, and even lack of sufficient water supply. Other factors such as toxins, viruses, bacteria, other infections or metabolic disorders, and stressors can interfere with kidney function and precipitate a problem.

Visceral gout is most often seen during a necropsy and is difficult to diagnose in a living specimen. The most frequently seen sign of the disease is sudden death. The symptoms, if there are any, are vague and non-specific and can include depression, lethargy, anorexia, feather plucking, or other behavioral changes. Absent definitive symptoms, uric acid levels can be routinely monitored. If the levels become elevated, an endoscopic procedure can diagnose gout.

If it is diagnosed in a living specimen it is diffi-cult, if not impossible, to treat and the prognosis is poor. Visceral gout cannot be "cured" but it can be managed to some extent and steps can be taken to prevent further uric acid build up. Exercise is important in treating the problem. Other treat-ments can include a diet heavy on the natural vegetable, fruits and Vitamin A and low in pro-tein. There are some allopathic drugs that can lower uric acids levels and have been used in birds with varied results. There are also several homeo-pathic treatments that might prove useful in man-aging this disorder.

While high protein levels have been associated with visceral gout, there is no evidence that healthy kidneys in a bird will be harmed by ex-cessive dietary protein. Birds in captivity; how-ever, are often exposed to a host of toxins and pathogens that unbeknownst to the owner can cause damage to their birds' kidneys. It is at that point that dietary protein levels become a poten-tial hazard.

While visceral gout is hard to detect and diffi-cult to treat once discovered, monitoring uric acid levels can be a useful tool for detecting and man-aging birds with this disorder. Annual check ups, plenty of clean fresh water and a well balanced diet are factors that can help keep your birds free of this disease.

Heavy Metal Toxicity

Lead and zinc are the two most common met-als that cause problems for pet birds. While trace amounts of heavy metals occur naturally and can be an essential part of the diet, when ingested outside of natural food sources, they are a potentially lethal problem. Lead is found in items throughout the household that birds might come into contact with and chew on. Zinc on the other hand usually comes from cage material or the hardware on toys. Birds need ingest only a small amount to create a big problem. The symptoms of heavy metal toxicity are nonspecific and can include lethargy, depression, anorexia, feather plucking, diarrhea, and in extreme cases, seizures and sudden death. Diagnosing metal poisoning in a bird is possible. X-rays will often show lead particles in the gizzard but zinc will not show up as readily. Blood work can help confirm the presence of zinc. Treatments vary depending on the type of metal ingested and the degree of toxicity. Lead poisoning might require surgery where as zinc might be treated with Chelation therapy. Chelation is the introduction of an agent that works with the structure of the metal to tightly bind it so that it may pass through the body. Calcium EDTA, administered either orally or by injection, is the most commonly used chelating agent.

Simple precautions can prevent metal toxicity in your bird. Birds are curious creatures and are drawn to bright, shiny objects. Monitor your bird's activity when it is not in its cage and pay attention to everything it puts in its beak. There are many sources of lead in your home including paint, weights in curtains, solder, and jewelry.

Zinc is often present in cage wires, especially if you are using a galvanized wire cage, as well as in the hardware used to hang toys. If the wire has been properly galvanized there should be no problem; however, examine the cage carefully before turning it over to your lory. Purchase material that has been galvanized after it has been welded. Make sure there are no bubbles or flaky areas. Remove any white oxidation that appears on the cage, as that will contain zinc and can be easily ingested. Clean the cages well with a fiber brush and a mildly acetic cleaner such as vinegar, which will impede the oxidation process. Never use a wire brush because it will scratch the surface.

Feather Plucking

There are few afflictions that are as puzzling and as frustrating as feather plucking. The problem occurs in all commonly kept parrot species and lories are no exception. The destruction of feathers can range from just a few missing feathers around the ankles to such extensive destruction that the follicles are damaged and the feathers never grow back. In some instances, the cause of feather damage can be readily identified. The cause can be chronic heavy metal toxicity, giardia, or a disease such as gout. It can also be a result of boredom or loneliness. At the first sign of feather damage, a veterinarian should see the bird. Before going any further into investigating the cause, a complete work up with blood tests and radiographs should be conducted. Never accept the answer that your bird is just hormonal and wants to breed. Indeed, that can account for some feather picking behavior but more often than not, there is an underlying, more serious cause. Failure to investigate might cost the bird its life. Once physical maladies have been ruled out, consider whether environmental factors might be causing a problem. Each bird is different in its perception and reaction to a cage location, stressors, or threats. Birds sitting by a big picture window might enjoy the view or the larger birds outside might constantly terrorize them. Since lories are naturally prey animals, it would be reasonable for them to fear hawks. Is there a heavy smoker in the household? Even if that person does not smoke indoors, the residue on their hands might irritate the bird. Is there a new love interest, baby, cat, dog, or bird? Dramatic changes in the environment can cause frustration and feather destruction. Is the cage in an area of heavy traffic? Constant activity near the cage might startle the bird constantly. Is the home too dry and does the bird have an opportunity to bathe regularly? If the environment seems just right, the cause for plucking could be a substitution for another behavior that your bird is not able to exhibit. In the wild, lories are highly social and very active birds. Lack of interaction with other birds or the human flock can lead to behavior problems that include feather plucking. If the bird is bored or lonely, a larger cage with perches on different levels and plenty of toys might help. Lack of exercise, which often goes hand in hand with boredom, can also lead to the destruction of feathers. Birds set up for breeding have on occasion plucked each other. Initially, feathers might be used to line a nest; however, the behavior can continue beyond the breeding season.

There are some who believe if a physical problem is diagnosed and treated, or the environmental factor removed, the feather plucking behavior will disappear. Conventional wisdom has shown that this is not always true. If a bird has destroyed its feathers for a long time, the behavior may become habitual and breaking the habit may be one of the biggest challenges you face as a bird owner. Never scold or punish your lory for destroying its feathers as you could destroy the relationship you have developed with the bird. Even though your bird looks a bit scruffy, bald birds are just as lovable as any other.

Parasitic Infections

There is no way to make these problems interesting to the reader but parasitic infections are conditions that lory owners should be aware of. Included in this category are Giardia and Trichomonas, both flagellate (that means these one celled rascals have tails) protozoa that affect the digestive system. Both Trichomonas and Giardia can be transmitted through direct contact or from food or water contaminated by infected feces. Adult birds can easily pass it on to their chicks during feeding.

Giardia is frequently found in budgerigars (parakeets) and cockatiels, which suggests that these birds are carriers. Although giardia may be present in a bird, there might not be obvious symptoms. When symptoms do occur they include runny droppings that might have an unpleasant odor, lethargy, weight loss, and yeast infections. Giardiasis may also cause feather plucking. These parasites form cysts, which are passed in the feces. These cysts can cause infection if passed along to other birds. These cysts can live outside the host for a couple of weeks so cage cleanliness is important in keeping parasitic infections under control.

Coccidia parasites have shown up often in lories. These parasites rarely cause problems in a normal, healthy bird that is kept in a clean and uncrowded environment. One such coccidian parasite is sarcocystis, which can be deadly. Parrots from Africa, Australia, and Asia seem to be more susceptible than those from the Americas. Birds most at risk are those which are kept outdoors in areas where there are opossums. Opossums shed the parasite through their feces. Cockroaches then consume the fecal material and, in turn, come into contact with and are eaten by the birds. Constructing cages and aviaries in such a way that opossums do not have access to the enclosures is effective prevention. If detected in time, it can be treated.

Fungal Infections

The most common fungal infections are candidiasis and aspergillosis. Candida, a yeast infection, is usually found in the digestive tract. In young chicks it is often referred to as "sour crop" or "slow crop." In adults it often presents as "cotton mouth," referring to the whitish build up of

mucous around the beak. In humans, we call it
"thrush." Candida is part of the normal digestive
flora; however the flora can become unbalanced,
as is often the case with a regimen of antibiotics,
and the presence of candida can increase. Because of the nature and contents of their diet,
lories can be quite susceptible to candida. Yeast
infections can be diagnosed with a fecal gram stain
and can be treated with medications such as nystatin. Many vets will prescribe nystatin prophy-
lactically when they are treating another infection with antibiotics. Nystatin is a fairly safe drug
and is not particularly toxic.

Aspergillosis usually affects the respiratory
system and is the result of inhaling the fungal
spores. It can be either a chronic or acute infection and can cause sudden death. It is an oppor-
tunistic infection and frequently appears when a
bird has a compromised immune system. Aspergil-
lus occurs naturally in most environments but
can flourish in the right kind of environment.
Moist bedding and mold can create that kind of
environment so take care to ensure that when
bedding and substrate in cages, nest boxes, or
play areas becomes damp and soiled it is removed
immediately. Corncob bedding is reputed to be a
great breeding ground for mold and fungus and
should not be used with lories. Aspergillosis can
cause difficulty breathing, weight loss, wheezing,
and lethargy. Diagnostic methods include blood
tests and fungal cultures. It can be a tenacious
infection, making treatment with antifungal medications difficult. Good husbandry practices will
reduce the risk of aspergillosis.

Bacterial And Viral Infections

Psittacine Beak and Feather disease (PBFD), or Psittacine Circovirus, was first discovered in Australia and is now found in psittacine flocks everywhere. Lories are very susceptible to this disease. This virus attacks the cells of the feathers and beak as well as some internal organs. If the virus does not cause the death of an infected bird, secondary infections resulting from a compromised immune system might. Symptoms of this disease include abnormal feather growth and loss, lesions beneath the surface of the skin, or overgrowth of the beak; however not every infected bird will immediately show signs. It can be spread through direct contact by ingesting or inhaling infected dust or fecal material. The virus can remain present outside of a host for many months. The incubation period for this virus can range from three weeks to several months or even years. While there are accurate tests to diagnose the disease, there is no known treatment. It is not known for certain whether all infected birds will die, as it seems some are able to clear the infection and develop a natural immunity or build up the necessary antibodies to fight the infection. Birds who are infected, or are even suspected of being infected should be isolated from healthy birds.

In the mid to late 1990s it was thought by some researchers that the virus had mutated into a variant, Psittacine Circovirus II, which was found in lories. Because this strain appeared to be biologically different, some tests did not detect it, causing negative test results in infected birds. This resulted in infected lories being exchanged all over the country and were subsequently infecting other lories. This problem was as expensive as it was heartbreaking. Current tests for Circovirus are considered to be quite accurate.

West Nile Virus

West Nile Virus has spread across the Unites States, causing concern for many exotic bird owners who have their birds outside some or all of the time. While it is possible for a parrot to be infected with this virus, the occasions of infection seem to be fairly rare. There are a number of different mosquito types and not every mosquito of every type carries this virus. Additionally only about 10% of the known carrier mosquitoes even carry the virus. In order for a bird to be infected it would then have to be bitten, most likely on the foot as the insects may have trouble getting through the feathers, by a mosquito carrying the virus. The likelihood of all these circumstances coming together at one time is very low. Additionally, parrots do not appear to be one of the birds most vulnerable to infection. During the first four years the disease was evident in the United States there were twelve documented psittacine deaths. In those few cases, the birds tended to be of South American or Australian origin. The benefits from exposing the bird to fresh air and sunshine far outweigh the risks associated with West Nile Virus infection. Companion parrots who do become infected and are otherwise healthy, can become subclinically infected, develop the appropriate immune response and clear the infection fairly quickly.

Mosquitoes are most prevalent during the early morning and the evening and precautions can be taken to minimize their number around your home. Remove all items such as bowls, flowerpots, and tires in which water can accumulate and stagnate. If you cannot remove items such as splash blocks for down spouts and pool covers, ensure they are emptied regularly. This will limit the places mosquitoes will lay their eggs. There are some products that can be used in your yard and can be obtained from your local hardware or garden store. One contains a compound known as methoprene; the other has permethrin. Methoprene is a synthetic growth hormone that interferes with the insect growth and development process. Permethrin is a broad-spectrum insecticide. Both use water as the delivery method and when used on calm days, are relatively harmless to birds; however, direct contact could cause problems. Deltamethrin is another pesticide that is relatively safe around birds. It is a synthetic insecticide whose structure is based on that of natural pyrethrin. Some communities spray for mosquitoes. Trucks are sent down the streets. Because the spray used is dense and does not become airborne, outdoor birds should be safe unless they are very close to the roadways.

Polyoma Virus

Polyoma virus affects primarily very young, newly hatched birds and can affect any type of parrot, including lories. An outbreak in a nursery can cause a high mortality rate among chicks, which can be financially devastating. It is believed that the virus can be transmitted through the egg. In young hatchlings, there are often no signs of illness. When symptoms are present, they generally include hemorrhaging and neurological impairment. In older birds whose immune systems are stronger, the incidence of infection is quite uncommon. The virus can cause mild transient infections that usually present as mild gastric upset. Adult birds are ordinarily able to clear the virus and develop a natural immunity.

The virus is resistant to many types of disinfectants; however, chlorine bleach is one of the agents that are effective against it. There is no known treatment for the virus but there is currently a vaccine available which is considered safe and effective. Because it is made from a killed virus, it does not infect the birds with the disease. Almost all birds vaccinated develop immunity to the virus. Because it is quite expensive and because the mortality rate in adult birds is low, often breeders and pet owners decline to provide it to their birds. Once administered, the vaccine will require periodic boosters to remain effective. The frequency of the booster depends on the risk factors involved, such as whether the bird stays the home or travels frequently to bird stores, bird clubs and other environments where there are other birds.

Psittacosis

Psittacosis, *Chlamydiaphila psittaci*, is a bacterial infection. Also known as Parrot Fever and

Chlamydiosis, Psittacosis is caused by one of several types of chlamydia organisms. Psittacosis is a zoonotic disease, which means humans can catch it from birds. Usually those humans who are susceptible to psittacosis are immune suppressed. Because the disease can be transmitted to humans, most states require veterinarians to report a psittacosis diagnosis in a bird to the local health department or other officials. According to the Centers For Disease Control and Prevention, since 1996, there have been fewer than fifty cases of psittacosis in humans in the United States reported each year. While this disease can be transmitted from parrots to humans, poultry is the most common cause of infection in human cases. The cases of human-to-human transmission are rare. Psittacosis in humans affects the respiratory system and the symptoms are similar to the flu. It is important to note that humans can be infected with other forms of chlamydia including a human strain or *C. felis*, a strain known to infect cats. Additionally, birds that test positive for chlamydia could possibly be infected with other forms as well. A blood test is necessary to diagnose the infection. The assays in a standard test will detect any known strain of the infection, not just *C. psittaci*.

Infection in birds usually occurs as a result of inhaled or ingested contaminated dust from feathers and fecal material. The bacteria can survive quite a long time apart from the host. Symptoms of Psittacosis include lethargy, diarrhea, labored breathing, and lime green or exceptionally dark droppings; however, infected birds can sometimes be asymptomatic. Treatment can be very successful but it does require approximately 45 days of treatment with an antibiotic such as tetracycline or doxycycline. Additionally, if there is more than one bird in the home, all of them should receive treatment even if test results are negative. Unlike other diseases, birds that clear a Psittacosis infection do not develop natural immunities so they can succumb to future infection. All known vertebrates are susceptible to some form of chlamydia. Following an outbreak of Psittacosis it will be necessary to thoroughly clean and disinfect cages, toys, and other items that have direct contact with the infected bird. A Psittacosis outbreak can be prevented with good husbandry practices, quarantining, and vet checking all new birds.

Proventricular Dilatation Disease

Proventricular Dilatation Disease or PDD, also called Macaw Wasting Disease, is fatal to birds. It affects the digestive tract, usually the crop and ventriculus, causing the muscles to atrophy. Classic signs of this disease include weight loss without loss of appetite, vomiting, and stools containing undigested food. Birds with advanced PDD may also show signs of central nervous system impairment such as lack of coordination or seizures. This disease has shown up not only in parrots but also in other non-psittacine birds such as Canadian geese. At this time there is no known treatment for this disease. Supportive care using human anti-inflammatory drugs known as COX-2 inhibitors has been effective in some cases but is still experimental. While research into this disease is ongoing, little is known about it. It is believed to be viral and the incubation period could be months or years. Diagnosis of this disorder on living specimens is often made on the basis of analyzing the symptoms and eliminating other maladies. A study of infected tissue, obtained through a crop biopsy, must be done in order to have a more certain diagnosis. While the disease can be transmitted from one infected bird to another, the method of transmission is not certain.

E. Coli And Other Bacteria

Escherichia (*E. coli*) is a bacterium that is part of a bird's normal intestinal flora and the amount present depends on the species of bird. It can be spread to birds by flies or through contact with contaminated food. Sprouted seeds purchased from the grocery store, fecal material, and rotting fruit are common sources of *E. coli* contamination. It can be diagnosed through a culture and treated with antibiotics and lactobacilli (probiotics). Keeping food and water free from fecal material and practicing good hygiene can prevent contamination. Be sure to wash your hands frequently when feeding birds and cleaning cages.

Other bacteria known to cause infections in lories include Klebsiella, Salmonella, Pseudomonas, Pasteurella, Mycobacterium (also known as Avian Tuberculosis), and Clostridium. None of them makes for terribly interesting reading material but sometimes it helps to have at least heard of them. Avian mycobacterium can be transmitted through contact with contaminated fecal material or soil. The infection can take a long time to develop and during that time the birds show no obvious symptoms of illness until the disease is quite advanced. Infected birds can show symptoms similar to PDD, where they lose weight. Treatment of infected birds is not recommended as this bacterium seems resistant to most drugs and effective treatment could take more than twelve months. Birds testing positive for mycobacteriosis should be either completely isolated or euthanized. To make matters worse, some strains of mycobacteria are zoonotic, meaning they can be transmitted from birds to humans. Salmonella is another bacterium that can cause problems in pet birds and it can be transmitted to humans as well. Birds can become infected as a result of eating contaminated food. It can also be passed to an unhatched chick through the shell. For some birds, it can be fatal; others can be carriers of salmonella for the remainder of their life. Clostridium is another type of bacteria that can remain viable for a long time in the environment – usually fecal material or soil. They are resistant to treatment but are not terribly common in pet birds.

Accidents And Hazards

Many pet lories have fallen victim to household accidents. The most common seem to be drowning in open toilets, getting stepped on, attacked by the family dog, or flying away. There are many simple things that can be done to help prevent tragedy. Remember, lories are incredibly curious creatures and they don't know what they might be getting into until it's too late. It is up to the human caretaker to be on guard and keep them as safe as possible. Always keep the lid down on the toilets, or better yet, the doors closed, lest someone forget to close the lid. Don't set up a situation where a bird could fly into an open pot or pan on your stove. If your lory is out of its cage, know where it is at all times. Wandering on the floor unattended can result in a horrible tragedy that will be tough to recover from. If there are other animals such as cats and dogs in the home, be extremely careful about letting them interact with your bird. Cats and dogs are predators and birds are prey animals. In a heartbeat, Fido or Fluffy may end up doing what comes naturally. And while they may not deliver a fatal attack, the bacteria in the mouths of these animals are highly toxic to birds. Ceiling fans are another household hazard. When operating, they can injure or kill a bird that accidentally flies into it. Window glass is yet another thing of concern. Most of us have seen or known of wild birds flying into picture windows or sliding glass doors. Your lory can do the same thing, often with tragic results. Make sure windows are covered or have decals on them or there is something to let the bird know it is solid. Birds that are unrestrained can and do fly off a shoulder no matter how well the wing feathers might be clipped. This is something to consider when taking a bird outside. Letting a bird chew on painted woodwork is risky. Aside from not helping the appearance of the home, unless you can be certain of the paint ingredients, you can assume it's toxic. Bird proofing the home should be done before the first bird is brought in. Beyond that, using common sense can be extremely helpful in preventing accidents.

Necropsies

A necropsy is the postmortem exam performed on a bird in order to determine the cause of death. In some cases a gross necropsy, which involves examining the bird for any obvious physical causes of death such as trauma injuries, lesions, or clear organ failure, is the only examination a vet will perform. While this might occasionally provide the cause of death, a full necropsy should be performed. A full necropsy usually includes a histopathology that studies tissue samples, hematology that tests the blood, viral and bacterial cultures, and toxicology. When a beloved bird dies it is hard to think about having a necropsy done but consider that it may be the only means by which we learn the true cause of the bird's death. The cause of death can be a mystery because it's hard to know when they're sick and the symptoms they often present are not indicative of one particular ailment. A necropsy will almost always clear up the mysteries. It can give us information on the cause of death and can in fact be the only way to diagnose some problems. We can determine what, if anything, we can do differently. When we know what happened we are better equipped to possibly prevent it from happening to our current or future birds. It can give us information so we can make positive changes. It affords the opportunity to learn and when we learn we can do a better job in the future. And even when the cause of death is obvious, as in the case of an accident, a check on the condition of the organs can provide valuable information. A necropsy can add to what little we already know and has the potential to advance the field of avian medicine and research. The benefits or having a necropsy done will almost always outweigh the cost.

Because bird emergencies and deaths never seem to occur during normal business hours, it is important to preserve the remains in the best way possible. Never freeze the body, as this will make it impossible to perform accurate tests on tissue and blood. Gently wet the body with warm soapy water, place it in a plastic bag and store in the refrigerator. This will help preserve it for a day or two, until it can be presented to a veterinarian. If you wish the remains to be returned to you after a complete necropsy is performed, be sure to advise the vet immediately. Receiving the remains back after the necropsy can be very difficult emotionally. Consider requesting the leg band be removed and returned to you instead.

Grooming

Wing FeatherClipping

Because some birds spend so much time out of their cages, many pet bird keepers feel it is essential to clip the bird's wing feathers. The purpose of this is not to prevent the bird from flying but to keep it from gaining altitude. Flying is good exercise for your bird; however, a fully flighted bird out of its cage can be at risk in the home environment. Certainly the biggest risk is when someone opens the door and the bird is able to glide into the big bad world out there. Even the most severe of trims might not prevent the bird from going aloft and landing in the tree-tops somewhere. There are additional risks inside the home when the bird is out of its cage. Open toilets, hot stovetops, windows, and ceiling fans all represent hazards to a flying bird.

Clipping wing feathers is not cruel; it does not hurt the bird. It is much like trimming hair and fingernails is for we humans. The chance for pain or injury comes when the flight feathers are not inspected closely prior to cutting them and a blood feather is involved. All new feathers start out with a blood supply and are encased in a sheath. As the feather grows, the blood supply withdraws and the sheath begins to crack, releasing the newly developed feather. If a blood feather is cut not only will the bird feel pain, there will also be bleeding. The clipping is not a permanent change. It will last only until the bird molts out the cut feathers. Under no circumstances should the tail feathers ever be clipped. Without the tail, the bird will have trouble balancing.

Clipping should only involve the primary flight feathers – the longest ones - and not the secondary feathers. The best trims occur when each feather is cut individually rather than cut as a row. While there are still references to the technique of trimming only one wing, this is generally not recommended. It causes the bird to be unbalanced and heightens the risk of injury from crashing into something during a flight attempt. Trim the feathers of both wings equally. When cutting the wing feathers, try to clip them far enough down that the ends do not stick out and annoy the bird.

A good feather clip will allow the bird to coast rather than crash. An unclipped bird requires vigilance and care. When the bird is out of its cage, the environment must be as bird-proof as possible. Draw curtains over those glass windows or doors. Turn the ceiling fan off. No bird should be out and unattended when household members are entering or leaving the home. If you're working at the stove, the bird should be in its cage.

Light birds such as cockatiels and cockatoos can fly even with what we consider to be a heavy clip. Stockier, wide-bodied birds like pionus parrots need fewer feathers trimmed. If too many feathers are removed there is a greater risk of injury such as a fractured keel bone or beak.

When undertaking the actually cutting, be careful holding and restraining the bird. Never forcibly pull the wing out and hold it that way. If the bird struggles, it is possible to fracture the wing bones.

There will be some who believe no bird should ever have the feathers trimmed and flight restricted. Certainly aviary birds need not be clipped. Most reputable breeders feel that fledglings should be allowed to learn to fly and land before their wing feathers are cut. Feather clipping is a personal choice.

If you are taking your bird outside, even the heaviest clips may not prevent tragedy. Never assume because you have ensured the wing feathers are cut that your bird is safe. If the bird becomes spooked it will fly off, seeking out the highest point possible. If it cannot fly up to the top of the tree, it will climb there. If there is the least bit of breeze, the bird can still coast and gain altitude, even with its wing feathers trimmed. Some bird owners have been able to train their pet bird to accept a harness and leash. If your bird is not one of those than it is wise to not take it outside unless it is caged or crated. And even tethered and caged birds are not without potential risk. Hawks flying overhead will consider your pet to be a tasty snack and may even grab it off the shoulder of its unsuspecting owner.

Nail Trimming

In the wild, normal perching and playing will keep a lory's toenails from getting too long. Life in a cage, often with smooth perches all of a similar size, eliminates some of these opportunities for naturally maintaining length and, as a result, the nails can become too long. No bird should be forced to cope with long or overgrown toenails. They can interfere with perching comfortably and they can get caught on cage wires and cause serious injury. There are several types of mineral and concrete perches designed to help file down nails while the bird perches on them. These special perches are available at most pet stores. Be sure you get a perch that is suited to the size of your bird's feet. It should be large enough that the bird cannot wrap its toes around it. Do not get sandpaper perch covers. They are not effective in trimming the nails and can cause problems for the bird's feet

If grooming perches are not working, it is time to take matters into your own hands and do the trimming yourself. At most pet stores and supply houses you can get a pair of scissors that look like little lobster claws, designed just for this purpose. A rotary sanding tool, such as a Dremel®, can also be quite useful for an avian manicure. When you attempt to do this yourself it might be wise to restrain the bird in a towel. Also have a small dish of cornstarch or some sort of clotting agent available. Do not trim too close to the quick as it will bleed and your bird will not enjoy it.

Beak Trimming

A bird's beak, like our own hair and nails, is constantly growing. Normal activities such as climbing and chewing will keep a bird's beak filed down properly. Although some parrots such as pionus have what seems to be an oversized upper mandible, an overgrown beak is generally a sign of an underlying health problem. If your bird's beak has grown longer than normal, make an appointment with your veterinarian. The overgrowth is often an indication of a liver problem.

Do not attempt to trim the bird's beak yourself. This is a task that should best be left to an experienced avian veterinarian. Attempts by bird owners can result in injury to the bird or worse. Unlike the toenails, a bird's beak has nerve endings and a blood supply fairly close to the tip.

Emergencies

First Aid

Have a first aid kit or first aid supplies on hand for emergencies. Keep it in a place near the birds and where it can easily be obtained when you are otherwise too frantic to think clearly.

The following are some basic first aid items every bird owner should have available:

A clean towel
Tuberculin (1 cc) syringes (no needles)
An electrolyte solution
Net
Heating pad
Tub, aquarium, or other vessel that can be made into a heated brooder
Disinfectant solution such as Betadyne™
Cornstarch (great for broken blood feathers or toe nails)
Needle nose pliers or forceps (good for pulling broken blood feathers)
Carrier, crate, or something to transport a sick or injured bird
An accurate gram scale that weighs in one-gram increments or less
Band Aids for yourself

Using A Towel To Restrain

In an emergency situation pet birds can sometimes be difficult to handle. Often, as in the case of manicures, they just do not want to sit there long enough to allow all eight nails to be trimmed. In these cases, a towel makes a good restraining device. A hand or medium sized towel is just the right size for lories. If you are able to pick up the bird, hold it close to your body, facing you, and gently wrap the towel around its body, starting around the neck. Once the towel is wrapped around the bird, it is effectively restrained. Always remain calm and handle the bird gently. Take care not to wrap the bird too tightly and do not apply too much pressure on the chest area as you could suffocate it. If you are unable to hold the bird to restrain it, you need to become a little creative in catching the bird with the towel. It helps to periodically have your bird play games with a towel so it does not become frightened when it sees you with one.

Some Common Household Emergencies

Emergencies tend to make us panic and when we panic our thought process is less clear. We then place stress on ourselves that in turn places stress on our birds. This is not intended to be the ultimate reference and should never be used as a substitute for veterinary care and knowledge; however, it can be helpful to know how to handle these situations as they arise.

Egg Binding

Mature female birds often decide to lay eggs even in the absence of a mate. Normally this is perfectly safe however every once in a while a problem can occur. Egg binding is what happens when a developed egg cannot be properly passed. Problems are more likely to occur in hens that are chronic egg layers but it can also happen even in birds that are laying for the first time. The process of laying eggs can deplete the bird's supply of calcium and protein. If the diet lacks sufficient quantities of these nutrients, the bird will not have sufficient nutritional resources for proper egg development. Signs of egg binding can include lethargy, weakness, fluffed feathers, straining, and changes in the droppings. In cases where the egg has properly developed, it can be felt in the hen's abdomen. If the shell is too soft, it might not be as evident by feel but the abdomen should still be somewhat soft and swollen. The problem can sometimes be alleviated by very gently placing the bird in a warm (85°F), dark and humid environment. This can be accomplished by assembling the container or aquarium and the heating pad. Place a cup of warm water inside the container with the bird. Put a rolled up washcloth in the water with about one third of it extended out of the cup. After a couple of hours the egg will hopefully pass. If these attempts fail and the hen has not passed the egg, it will be necessary to obtain veterinary care. Egg binding can become a serious, life-threatening problem if the egg cannot be passed or if it breaks internally.

Broken Blood Feathers

Developing feathers are encased in a sheath with a blood supply. As the feather develops the blood supply diminishes; however, every once in a while fresh blood feathers can get broken. Broken blood feathers are common after a night fright where the bird has been flapping frantically in the cage. While the bleeding caused by breaking blood feathers is not usually sufficient to cause harm to the bird, sometimes it's just better to be safe than sorry. There are two ways to deal with the problem. Gently restrain the bird in a towel keeping in mind it might not be totally awake, and apply cornstarch to the area around the break. Packing on some cornstarch can expedite clotting. If that fails, the feather can be pulled. Using the needle nose pliers or forceps, pull the broken feather straight out. Don't be squeamish. While it may not be comfortable for the bird, it probably bothers you more. Once the feather is removed, the bleeding should cease.

Other Bleeding

Blood is usually a sign of an emergency. First, before you panic, find out what part of the bird is bleeding and why. Birds can lose a larger percentage of their blood volume than can mammals; however, keep in mind that because of their size they don't have vast quantities of it. If the blood you find is in the cage and on the perches and it appears to be dry, watch the bird closely for a couple of hours to ensure the bleeding has truly stopped and to make sure there are not other problems. If the bird becomes lethargic, weak, or shows difficulty breathing, contact your vet. Consult a vet immediately in the case of cat bite wounds whether they are bleeding or not. If the bird is bleeding as a result of small cut, use a gauze pad or clean cloth and apply gentle but direct pressure to the wound. Once bleeding has stopped, the cut can be cleaned using diluted hydrogen peroxide or something similar. Applying cornstarch or styptic powder can stop bleeding from broken nails. Beaks have a blood supply very close to the tip and occasionally they get injured and bleed. Pack the area with cornstarch or styptic powder. Applying gentle, direct pressure might also work. If the beak is actually broken, contact a vet. Do not be alarmed if your bird is a little hesitant about eating after a beak tip injury. The area might be a bit sensitive for a day or two so avoid hard foods during that time.

Night Frights

Night frights are what we call those occasions when something startles your bird in the middle of the night and sends into a flapping, squawking panic while it is not quite awake. The state the bird is in at that point is much like a human when they are sleepwalking. This is one of those occasions when a towel is useful. When you find your bird having a night fright try not to wake it up suddenly. Turn on a light so both of you can see. Gently wrap the flailing bird in the towel keeping in mind that it might bite you without realizing it is doing so. Once you have collected your bird in a towel just hold it and talk quietly to it until it is completely awake. Check for any broken blood feathers and, if present, treat accordingly. If the bird is prone to night frights perhaps the cage should be moved. The bird may be reacting to something environmental. I once had a bird prone to terrible night frights. One restless night lead me to discover that in the middle of the night my newspaper was being delivered and the headlights shining in the window startled the bird. Moving his cage stopped the problem immediately. Using a night light might also help.

Dehydration

This can occur when birds are using water bottles that have not been checked daily. The inquisitive lory might enjoy stuffing pieces of food into the stopper until it is no longer a source of water. Because of their diet, of which a large percentage is nectar and fruit, dehydration is not as common in lories as it can be in other types of parrots. But if your lory eats primarily the dry powder or pellets, it will need a lot of water. Insufficient water supply can not only cause dehydration but also lead to problems involving the liver and kidneys. If you do discover your bird is dehydrated, immediately administer an electrolyte solution, such as what is available for infants and children or popular types of sports drinks. This can revive the bird almost immediately. If it does not, the bird should be taken to a veterinarian immediately.

Cat And Dog Bites

Pasteurella bacteria are commonly found in the mouths of cats. Cat bites, even if the skin does not appear to be broken, should be considered serious and receive immediate veterinary attention. Birds who initially seem unaffected by an encounter with a cat can become suddenly and acutely ill and die very quickly. Pasteurella aside, puncture wounds as a result of a bite can develop infections rather quickly, making them a medical emergency.

Safe Or Not Safe?

A lot of what is considered safe and not safe is a matter of common sense. Birdproof your home in the same way you would childproof it for a toddler. Birds have a respiratory system made up of several air sacs. It is more delicate than ours and they are much smaller than we are. They can tolerate only a fraction of what we can. Fumes of all kinds can create problems for your bird and, not coincidentally, for yourself as well. Think twice about spraying perfume or hairspray in the same room with your bird. Consider boarding your birds when your house is being painted or new carpet is being laid. The propellants in aerosol cans can be toxic to birds. All of these things are essentially air pollutants that can be detrimental to your bird's health. While having a bird does not mean you must rid your home of all these things, limit the occasions for your bird to have direct exposure to them.

Some Common Household Toxins

- Apple seeds – Okay, not really. They contain tiny amounts of cyanide; however, your lory would have to eat an enormous quantity of them all at once in order to suffer any ill effects. The number of seeds a lory might encounter in on apple is not sufficient to cause harm.
- Avocado – There seems to be some question about the toxicity of avocado. Some claim it is harmful to parrots. Others claim that is an Urban Legend kept alive by the prevalence of the Internet. Most consistently seen is the statement that

the leaves, skins and pits are toxic but the actual fruit is not. Many bird keepers have safely fed avocado to their birds for years with no ill effects. While there seems to be a lack of evidence supporting an across-the-board claim of toxicity, why take a chance when there are so many other things you can offer.

- Caffeine and alcohol – These are human food items that should never be shared with your lory no matter how much it wants them. Both are potentially lethal.

- Chocolate - It contains theobromine, which can be deadly if consumed in a large enough quantity.

- Cigarette smoke – It's not even good for us.

- Cleaning agents - Includes soap, cleansers, bathroom cleaners, oven cleaners, and full strength bleach. If you use any of these to clean your bird's cage, do so when your bird is out of its cage and be sure they are thoroughly rinsed away before putting the bird back in. Both the cleaning agents themselves and their fumes can be toxic.

- Cosmetics, fragrances, nail polish and remover and other toiletries - Many of these items that we use daily and take for granted can be toxic in some form to birds. While the use of them may not be harmful, do not allow your lory to come into direct contact with them. Do not use hair spray or other aerosols in the same room your bird is in. Both the ingredients and the propellants can be toxic. Deodorant, nail polish, acetone and perfume can all contain harmful and even deadly components.

● Non-stick cookware – This stuff is coated with a substance called PTFE. If heated above 500° F it can release deadly fumes. If you are the kind of person who is apt to go away and forget to turn the burner off after you've finished cooking, you might want to invest in some different pots and pans. Or, maybe you don't belong in the kitchen at all.

● Pesticides – They kill pests don't they?

● Scented Candles and Air Fresheners – There is some indication that the essential oils used in these items can be toxic to birds. To be safe, do not burn them. If you must, do so only in a well-ventilated area, as far away from your bird as possible.

Flowers

Lories love flowers. They are physiologically designed to obtain nutrition from them. There are many flowers that are safe for your bird under certain circumstances. Flowers that have been sprayed with pesticides or are growing on trees that have been fertilized and sprayed within the last six months or so are not so good for them. Do not use flowers from nurseries, garden centers

Red Lory with Hibiscus flower. Photo by Matt Schmit

and florists. The chemicals used during the growing process can be highly toxic. Before giving flowers to your bird, know where they came from and if you have any reason to believe they have been treated with anything, do not use them. Your best bet is to grow them yourself so you know they are safe.

Some common flowers your lory will love: Acacia, Bottlebrush, Calendula, Carnation, Daisies, Dandelion, Hibiscus, Honeysuckle, Marigolds, Milk Thistle, Nasturtiums, Pansies, Passionflowers, Roses, Sunflowers, and tree flowers including apple, citrus, and eucalyptus.

Note: While many flowers may be safe, other parts of the plant including, leaves, stems and roots may be toxic

A partial list of safe plants and trees: Acacia, African Violet, Alder, Ash, Aspen, Baby's Tears, Bamboo, Begonia, Birch, Bougainvillea, Chickweed, Christmas Cactus, Cissus/Kangaroo vine, Coleus, Cottonwood, Corn Plant, Crabapple, Dandelion, Dogwood, Donkey Tail, Eucalyptus, Ferns (Asparagus, Birds Nest, Boston, and Maidenhair), Figs, Gardenia, Grape Ivy, Grape Vines, Guava, Hawthorne, Hens and Chickens, Jade Plant, Kalanchoe, Magnolia, Manzanita, Marigold, Monkey Plant, Mother-In-Law Tongue, Mulberry, Nasturtium, Natal Plum, Norfolk Island Pine, Palms (Areca, Date, Fan, Lady Parlor, Howeia, Kentia, Phoenix, Sago), Pepperomia, Petunia, Pine, Pittosporum, Poplar, Prayer Plant, Purple Passion, Rubber Tree, Schefflera, Sensitive Plant, Spider Plant, Spruce, Swedish Ivy, Sweet Gum, Thistles, Umbrella Plant, Velvet Nettles, Wandering Jew (green, variegated and purple), White Clover, Willow, Zebra Plant.

Some Not–So-Safe-Plants

The following is a partial list of plants that may be considered unsafe for a variety of reasons. Some may contain toxins that, when ingested in large quantities, can cause digestive problems or skin irritation. Others may be highly toxic in their entirety or some element of the plant may be toxic:

Amaryllis, Azalea, Black Locust, Box Elder, Buttercup, Cactus (danger from thorns), Caladium, Cedar, Clover, Coffee Tree, Crocus, Dieffenbachia, Elderberry, Gingko, Hemlock, Holly, Iris, Laurel, Lily, Marijuana, Milk Weed, Mimosa, Mistletoe, Morning Glory, Mushrooms, Orchid, Oleander, Olive, Ornamental Ivy, Philodendron, Poison Ivy, Poppy, Pothos, Privet, Ragweed, Rhododendron, Trumpet Vine, Verbena, Wisteria

The bark and sap of some hardwood trees might be unsafe for birds so it is essential to do your research before using them.

Also not safe are the bulbs of flowers such as tulips, jonquils, hyacinths, daffodils, and iris.

Note: Nightshade is a group of plants whose members can be highly toxic; however there are some safe and edible members of this family. Potatoes, tomatoes, and eggplant are all edible; however, the leaves, roots and vines may not be. All parts of Belladonna can be deadly poisonous.

Chapter 5
FREQUENTLY ASKED QUESTIONS

What's the difference between a lory and a lorikeet?

None really. The terms are interchangeable and using either is correct. The term "lorikeet" is often used when referring to the smaller species that generally have long, pointed tails. The term "lory' is often used to describe those larger birds with shorter, rounder tails.

How can I get my lory to try new foods?

Lories are naturally curious creatures and it's this trait that makes introducing new things fairly easy. A little patience and consistency might be required. Offer the new items to your lory every day, not just sporadically. Ultimately it will get used to seeing these things and will start sampling.

My lory begs at the table. Is it safe to give her table scraps?

Moderation is the key to managing most situations. Most human foods in very small quantities will be fine for your lory. Bits of pasta, rice, and vegetables without butter or salt, and pizza crusts will not harm them. You might want to limit their opportunities to snack on rare beef but they may enjoy trying to extract the marrow from a chicken bone (with supervision of course). Sharing your meal should never be a significant portion of the lory's total diet. Just as important as the food you're offering at the table is considering whether you want to develop the habit of having your bird on your dinner plate regularly. Remember your company may not enjoy this as much as you do.

At what age will my lory start to talk?

This depends on so many factors. Many lories will start to imitate speech the sounds in its environment shortly after weaning. Some lories will never talk and some will only imitate sounds rather than speech. Every bird is an individual and unique in what it does and how it does it. If talking is an essential element of bird ownership you might wish to consider a different type of bird. Many lories can say a few words by the time they are a year old, if not before.

I've been told my lory should not sit on my shoulder because that is a position of dominance. Is that correct?

Birds are perceived as being dominant because it makes sense to us humans. Dominance tends to be more of a mammal trait than a bird trait. Dogs, with whom we have shared our lives for centuries, have issues with dominance and we are quite accustomed to that. A flock is different from a pack and bird hierarchies tend to be structured a bit differently. Lories do not have an "alpha" or flock leader bird. They take turns with such tasks as sentinel duty. These lookout birds will often sit at the highest point because that affords the best view of threats and danger. But the positions constantly change and no one bird seems to be on guard duty very long. Birds who have bonded to one another sit side by side at eye level with each other. It is not unusual for your bird to feel comfortable at eye level with the human it has bonded to. It is also not peculiar to think that your bird, after sitting comfortably on your shoulder, might not want to go back in its cage. The same bird might be just as resistant if it had been sitting on your lap or on a play stand. There is one big risk associated with keeping a bird on your shoulder and that is being bitten on the face.

My lory has laid an egg but she does not have a mate. What should I do?

Leave the egg and let her sit on it. Either she will get bored and abandon it shortly after laying, or abandon it when she instinctively knows the natural incubation time is up. Removing the eggs soon after they are laid might just encourage her to lay another one. Intermittent egg laying is not unusual in hens that have reached sexual maturity. Excessive egg laying can be detrimental to her health. And do not be alarmed if when she is done brooding, she consumes the egg. This is natural.

Can two different kinds of lories mate and produce offspring?

Yes they can. Not only can they produce offspring, those birds can be fertile and produce their own offspring. Some hybrids occur naturally in the wild but the vast majority of the ones we see are "man-made." The issue of hybridizing is primarily a moral one and most serious aviculturists oppose it. Lories are such beautiful creatures just the way they are; hybridizing will not produce anything that comes close to being as beautiful. Hybrid lories make just as good companion birds as any other; however, most responsible bird owners will ensure they will not end up in a breeding situation.

How long will my lory live?

Because lories have only been kept as pets in captivity for a relatively short time, it is hard to know exactly what their life expectancy is. Kept in aviaries with plenty of exercise, fresh air, and sunshine it is possible they will live even longer than inside our homes. House lories can fall victim to myriad household accidents so when the bird is out of its cage it should be supervised and not left alone. With the right diet, vigilant monitoring, and the opportunity to get regular exercise, it's reasonable to expect your lory to live between ten and twenty years.

I'm getting a second lory. Can I put it in the same cage with my first lory?

Unless you are planning to breed them, it would be better to house birds in separate cages. Birds, when placed together, will often form a bond with each other that is stronger than the one they have with you. Housing your lories together might jeopardize your relationship with them individually. Also lories can be very aggressive or territorial. If unable to escape the cage, one of them could end up seriously injured or dead. This can happen so quickly that even if you witness it you may not be able to intervene in time.

Will my lory get along with my other bird?

Lories are very aggressive birds and because of their fearless nature it is not a good idea to let them interact directly with other birds, even other lories, without close supervision. It is quite possible that your lory will assert itself with any other bird, regardless of the size difference, and it only takes a split second for a serious injury to occur.

Are there some lory species that are more easygoing or less aggressive than others?

Lories by their very nature are aggressive birds. It is very hard to stereotype a particular species of bird. That being said, many people who have kept a variety of different lories indicate that the birds in the *Chalcopsitta* genus (black, duyvenbode's, cardinal, yellow streak) are calmer and easier going than most others. With the Rainbow lories, Green Napes are said to become quite nippy whereas Edwards are said to be the gentlest of the group.

Why can my bird eat things like hot peppers without seeming to have a problem?

Parrots lack the receptors in their nerve endings that react to the peppers. They do not feel the same hot, burning sensation we do when we eat them, specifically, the seeds of the peppers. Be careful when you come into contact with your bird's beak after it has consumed a hot pepper because you will most certainly feel the sizzle your bird cannot experience. To add insult to injury, parrots also do not have nearly as many taste buds as do mammals so they are less sensitive to many flavors than humans.

I'd like to offer my lory flowers to eat and play with. How can I find out if they are safe?

In addition to the safe flowers listed in this book, there are many information sources available. In the case of safe flowers and plants, the Internet is a good resource.

I am painting and/or having a new carpet/floor installed in my home. Can the fumes be dangerous to my lory?

Yes the fumes can be a potential hazard. Rather than trying to determine if particular fumes might be problematic, consider boarding your bird outside your home while the painting or carpet installation takes place. Be sure to air out your residence completely before bringing your lory back home.

I've heard that using non-stick cookware can kill my bird. Can I use it safely or not?

Non-stick cookware is coated with a chemical called PTFE. The fumes can be deadly at temperatures over 500° F. To be safe, do not house birds in the kitchen and never go away and leave your pots and pans on a source of heat. Many cautious bird owners have stopped using non-stick surfaces in order to provide a safer environment.

What about air fresheners and cleaning products? Scented candles?

Essentials oils, which are often used for the scent, have fumes that are believed to be toxic to birds. You can create your own natural and safe air freshener or potpourri using items such as cinnamon. Unscented beeswax candles can provide a safer alternative if you desire that candle-lit ambience.

Should I give my lory vitamins in addition to its regular diet?

No. If you are feeding a balanced diet and including one of the commercial products for lories, you are giving the bird the vitamins and minerals it needs. Too many vitamins can actually cause health problems for birds.

Should I provide my lory with a nest box or hut for sleeping?

Unlike many other parrots, lories like to sleep or roost inside some sort of enclosure. They will readily accept almost anything from a traditional nest box to a tissue box to a hammock or tent type thing. Even lories that are not set up for breeding prefer to sleep "inside" so consider providing your bird with its own little sleeping place.

My lory sometimes grumbles in a low voice and I cannot make out what he is saying. What does that mean?

It means he is trying to talk. Often birds will mimic the cadence of human speech before they ever clearly utter any words. Some birds living in households where they listen to a lot of conversation will mumble in a way that sounds like conversation or the television.

Help— my lory is a monster! Ok, so he's more like an out of control 2 yr. old. Where do I start in teaching him manners so he's more manageable?

One of the reasons we have lories is because they have that indomitable spirit. But that spirit can be a handful at times. Your bird does need boundaries and guidelines. One of the first things you can teach your lory is the "step up" command. That forces the bird to step onto your finger in order to come out of its cage or to be transported elsewhere. Even with the youngest bird, it is best to teach your bird this when you first get it rather than waiting until there is a problem. Begin by gently pressing your index finger on the bird's legs or abdomen and say "step up." The bird will get the idea fairly soon. Then each time you open the cage or go to pick it up, you extend your index finger to it, repeat the words, and let it step onto your finger. Be sure to praise the bird when you get the desired reaction and never scold it when it forgets to obey. For many birds and their owners, the step up action is practically second nature. There are other ways to train parrots using praise and rewards. Clicker training is one of the more popular techniques. First used for obedience training dogs, it has been effective with parrots as well. Be mindful of your bird's attention span as it isn't terribly long and if the bird is not enjoying the activity it will cease participating.

My lory has suddenly started delivering painful bites. We're afraid or unwilling to handle him now. What can we do about it?

Lories tend be excitable birds, easily getting wound up and sometimes cascading out of control. Many "bird behaviorists" claim that lories are the one type of parrot that do not give some indication of their intent to nip. In some instances, a lory may bite as a result of aggression or territorialism. Other times it may bite out of excitement. When dealing with an unpredictable bird, be calm and gentle with your approach. Speak quietly and, if you are bitten, try not to scream, curse, or fling the bird across the room. Some lories go through a phase referred to as "the terrible two's" and it is during this period that bites might become a problem. It has been my experience that these bouts of bad behavior do not last very long. Sometimes it helps to re-

move the bird from its cage and take it to somewhere neutral or outside its normal environment,
like to a different room in the house, where you
can sit and hold it. Sometimes the bird is biting
you for a reason and it is up to you to figure out
why. Have you changed something like your hair,
eyeglasses, or the location of the cage? Have you
added a new family member or pet? If the reasons for the bites are environmental you may be
able to make some changes that will help your
bird adjust. If this is the case, try contacting some
lory owners for their advice and suggestions.

Is it possible to "potty train" my lory?

Yes it is and many people have managed to do
so with a fair amount of success. Potty training
will follow a routine similar to other types of training where the bird is taught to associate a particular command or even a location with a certain
behavior and the appropriate behavior is rewarded. Because lories tend to "go" more often
than other birds, you should allow a potty break
every five or so minutes.

Yellow-bibbed Lory

Chapter 6
LORIES – THE FAMILY LORIIDAE

Endangered Species

Lories, as is the case with almost all parrots, are endangered species. The Convention on International Trade in Endangered Species, better known as CITES, developed in 1973, is an international agreement between governments of various countries. Because the plant and animal trade crossed the borders of many countries, there was a need to protect some species through the cooperation of the countries involved. Trade includes not just live specimens but also a variety of products, goods, and medicines made from certain animals or plants. The purpose of the agreement is to ensure that the international trade of animals does not in any way threaten their survival.

Formed in 1973, adhering to the agreement is voluntary. While legally binding between the parties it does not replace the national laws of individual countries. It does however lay the foundation for domestic legislation. There have not been many species protected by CITES become extinct since the convention began. It protects more than 30,000 plant and animals species.

The species protected by CITES are listed on three appendices, determined by the level of protection needed. Appendix I includes the most vulnerable species; those facing an extremely high risk of extinction. Trading in these species is generally prohibited except under certain circumstances. Appendix II includes species that are not imminently threatened with extinction but may become so if the trade is not closely controlled. Appendix III is a list of species protected in at least one country which has asked other CITES Parties for assistance in controlling the trade. These are the least threatened of all. Species on Appendix I and II may only be added or removed through the meeting of the Convention. Species on Appendix III may be added or removed at the request of an individual government. All but two lories are classified as Appendix II on the CITES endangered species list. The Red-and-blue lory, *Eos histrio*, and the Ultramarine Lory, *Vini ultramarina*, are classified as Appendix I.

Several factors are responsible for the population decline. One of the largest is the destruction of natural habitat and nesting sites. As logging, mining, farming, and civilization encroach, the natural forests are being destroyed. Many of the countries where lories are found have extreme poverty. Clearing land for grazing livestock and growing crops is one of the ways people are able to survive and take care of their families. Another byproduct of the poverty that threatens the bird population is hunting. Because the exotic bird market worldwide is a vast and lucrative one, the local people can feed their families on the proceeds from selling desirable birds. They do not take kindly to the interference of outsiders, no matter how well intentioned. The birds, along with other fauna and flora, are part of each country's natural resources and presumably available to the citizens to utilize. It is hard for many of us to envision losing these beautiful birds forever but the poverty experienced in some of these countries probably exceeds our wildest imagination. Without finding suitable methods for relieving poverty and suitable alternatives to hunting or destroying the habitats, the native birds' existence will continue to be threatened.

Conservation And Preservation

According to Webster's Dictionary, conservation is the planned management of natural resources to prevent exploitation, destruction, or neglect. Many people believe that by breeding rare or endangered species, they are assisting conservation efforts. While working with these types of birds can be an important mission, it should not be mistaken for conservation. The concept of breeding for a particular purpose brings up the issue of conservation versus preservation. Preservation is to keep safe from injury, harm, or destruction. Breeding endangered birds that are likely to become extinct in their native habit, in our lifetime, is preserving the species. The vast majority of birds bred in captivity are not likely to be released into the wild to add to the existing populations nor are they likely to have any impact on the existing wild populations. With the loss of so many habitats, it might even be impossible to introduce captive raised birds back into the wild. This is not to say that captive breeding does not have its place in aviculture or in the future of certain birds. Species that are disappearing from their native habitat might become completely extinct if there is no captive breeding. While they may never fly free in their native land, captive breeding might keep these birds from disappearing completely. It would be more accurate to say these birds are being bred for preservation.

The efforts that can be made on behalf of conservation are not so obvious. If birds reared in captivity are not likely to be released into their wild habitats, what can be done to promote conservation? Conservation efforts must help the birds in the wild, or at the very least, offer some economic relief to the country of origin. When setting up a private or a cooperative breeding program, some of the profits could be sent to the country of origin to help maintain a habitat, provide artificial nest sites, or other programs to benefit the native birds. Ecotourism is an example of how a particular country can be helped. Tourist dollars are poured into the local economy while promoting pride in rather than destruction of their natural resources. If the human population is given the means to eat and survive, there may be less need to clear out habitats in order to have land for crops and grazing. There is controversy surrounding the benefits of ecotourism as a conservation tool. Some scientists feel that it causes more harm than good to the species involved. Having humans invade their habitat can cause stress to the protected fauna as well as damage to the native flora.

On a small scale, rearing birds for the pet trade in captivity, thus considerably reducing the need for wild caught birds could be considered a conservation effort. Using captive raised birds could reduce the need for capturing wild birds and reducing their existing populations. Contributing to conservation-based groups can be helpful but research very carefully any organization before you start writing checks. Their goals, expectations, and even methodologies might not be compatible with your own. Additionally, some organizations pass little if any of the monetary offerings into conservation programs, using the funds instead for administrative, advertising, legal fees and other costs.

Import And Export

Laws regarding the trade in native species, non-native species, and endangered species vary from country to country. Australia for example does not allow the export of its native species, even those commonly regarded as pests. Exportation stopped in the 1960s. Prior to that, however, it was common. The country did allow some legal importation of birds into the country in the mid 1990s. In addition to Australia, many other countries of origin have implemented restrictions on exportation of their native birds. In 1992, the United States passed the Wild Bird Conservation Act (WBCA) that stopped the general importation of CITES listed species and allowed legal importation only through cooperative breeding programs approved by the U.S. Fish and Wildlife Service. Thus far, the Solomon Island Parrot Consortium has managed to import Yellow-bibbed and Cardinal Lories into the United States. Europe has imposed import controls on many species of lory as well. In both the U.S. and Europe legal importation must not have an impact on the wild populations and the birds must be obtained legally. During the 1970s and 1980s, when many countries allowed legal import and export, a number of lory species were readily available. As a result, many populations became firmly established in aviculture. Because large numbers of captive raised lories are readily available and the availability keeps the prices reasonable, there is less need to take them from the wild.

Genus & Species

While there are approximately fifty three species of lory divided into twelve genera, only the captive lories found in the United States will be discussed in any detail. It is impossible to determine just what birds are being kept, and to what extent, as no census has ever been successfully taken. Occasionally it has been discovered that an aviculturist is keeping birds the rest of us have never seen.

Scientific nomenclature and taxonomy are not absolute. When ornithologists and researchers began studying, identifying, and classifying birds they did not have many of the tools available to them that we have now. Often birds were placed into certain classifications based on common traits. For example, all lories belong in the Class Aves (birds) and in the order Psittaciformes (parrots). Parrots are classified based on some very obvious features such as their hooked upper mandibles and zygodactyls toes (two going forward and two going back). In the order of Psittaciformes is the Family Loriidae, subfamily Loriinae and finally the genus and species. To make it just a little more confusing, within species are subspecies.

Lories are grouped together because of the traits unique to that group, the most notable of which is their brush tongue. Within the group, additional classifications were made to establish different genera. Often these classifications were made on the basis of similar physical traits. The classification of some was based on more detailed information such as range or anatomical traits. Taxonomists have not always agreed on classifications, especially when it has come to genus, species, and subspecies. As a result, not every reference will be the same. Several lories have been placed in one genus only to be moved to another. For example the Collared or Solitary Lory, the one bird placed genus *Phigys,* is believed by many to more correctly belong in the genus *Vini.* The Goldie's Lorikeet has found itself in both genus *Trichoglossus* and genus *Psitteuteles.*

The common names of birds vary from region to region. Knowing the most widely accepted scientific name of a bird can be helpful when communicating with others who are not familiar with a specific common name. Additionally, it helps clear up confusion with common names that sound similar. In the Genus *Amazona,* there is the Spectacled Amazon (*A. albifrons*) and the Red-spectacled Amazon (*A. pretrei*). Three birds commonly seen in the pet parrot trade have the word "dusky" in their common name. Dusky could be referring to a lory, a pionus or a conure. Scientific names are not an absolute certainty. A Blue-mountain lory is the same bird as the Swainson's (*Trichoglossus haematodus moluccanus*). With the advancements in science, the taxonomy is likely to change again. Research, some of which includes the study of lory DNA, may redefine the entire taxonomic structure of the family Loriidae.

Chalcopsitta

Lories in this group include the Black, Cardinal, Duyvenbode's, and Yellow-streaked. Members of this genus of lories are larger than most other lories, about twelve inches long and weighing in the neighborhood of 200 to 250 grams. They have long, rounded tails and are native to the lowlands of New Guinea and some nearby islands. For the moment they appear to be well established in their native habitat. Their wing beats are noticeably shallow and their flight seems slow. The most distinctive trait of this group is the bare skin surrounding the lower mandible. Their beaks are black, except for the Cardinal whose beak is only partially black, and they do not posses the same brightly colored plumage of some of the more commonly seen lories. In my opinion their subtle coloring makes them more beautiful. For anyone who is thinking about getting started with lories, the *Chalcopsitta* family will provide a richly rewarding avian experience. If I could only have one lory in the world I would narrow it down to a choice from this group. They are reputed to be some of the cuddliest lories and even breeder birds who were hand reared often retain their sweet disposition. Even some of the wild caught birds of this genus have been known to develop a good relationship with their human keepers.

As a whole, this group of lories seems to be the gentlest and best natured of the lories. These characteristics are documented as far back as one hundred years ago. In his 1896 book "The Loriidae," St. George Mivart declares that birds in this genus "...frequently approach the human habitations, which lead to their often being caught. Then they are easily domesticated and at least two species of them are said to be amongst the gentlest of birds." My experience with this genus indicates that this is a very accurate description of these birds; they are not the least bit shy. Of the *Chalcopsitta* group, Mivart additionally indicates that some "will spontaneously approach human dwellings, and in most of them make excellent pets, except for those persons who cannot tolerate the shrill cries they often emit."

One of the most overlooked lories has been the Black Lory, *Chalcopsitta atra*. Black Lories are commonly found in Irian Jaya, Western New Guinea. This bird is without a doubt one of the most delightful lories anyone could have. On first glance one might think it's just a black crow only with a hooked bill but closer examination reveals this is an incorrect assessment. While the bird is primarily black in color, there is a purple sheen to the feathers. Another look reveals subtle shades of yellow and red. Black lories are about 12 inches long and weigh in the neighborhood of 250 grams. While they are as noisy as any other parrot they can be gentle and affectionate. Of the Black Lory specifically, Mivart states "It seems to approach human habitation: hence it is often caught, when it is easily domesticated and shows itself gentle and attractive." While Blacks are not noted for being accomplished talkers and mimics, some can be very entertaining with their talking abilities and outgoing nature. Black lories may be one of the oldest documented lories. Both Mivart and Rosemary Low refer to a 1771 description of them in an account of a voyage to New Guinea by Sonnerat. They are relatively common in aviculture in the Unites States and appear less frequently in Europe and South Africa.

Yellow-streaked Lories, *Chalcopsitta scintillata*, have gained recognition as wonderful pets. They are native to southern New Guinea in Irian Jaya. These birds are the only members of the genus *Chalcopsitta* that have green plumage. Their wings and bodies are various shades of green, with red foreheads, thighs and breast, the back of the head and neck are streaked with bright yellow shafts. Their beaks are dark and their voices are quite harsh and high pitched. They are slightly smaller than the black lories. Owners of these lories describe them as generally sweet, very loving and good-natured but also indicate they often tend to be one-person birds. While these birds are often messy, owners feel they are worth the extra trouble because they are such loving pets. One man describes the normal greeting of his Yellow-streaked Lory as one that includes the entire body as if he is unable to contain his joy at seeing his human and he says it's a daily thrill to be the recipient of such a demonstration. Yellow-streaked Lories breed easily in captivity but they do tend to be a bit aggressive towards other birds and are not well suited to multi species lory aviaries or flock situations.

The Duyvenbode's or Brown Lory, *Chalcopsitta duivenbodei*, is another dramatically marked bird. Duyvenbode's are native to northern parts of New Guinea. The plumage is generally dark brown, highlighted with bright yellow on the thighs, forehead, around the beak and under the wings. Their beaks are also black. As pets, these birds have been described as sweet and devoted and tend to like most humans. They make excellent companion birds. They are typical lories so do not be surprised at the high-pitched shriek that is their voice. Duyvenbode's Lories are well established in aviculture in the Unites States, South Africa and Europe.

Their gregarious nature makes them well suited as companions. Once the captive populations become better established, more people will have the opportunity to keep these delightful lories.

Charmosyna

The fourteen lories in this genus include the Palm, Red-chinned, Striated, Wilhelmina's, Red-flanked, Duchess, Fairy, Josephine's and Papuan or Stella's Lorikeet. Lories in this group are very beautiful, quite small, and nearly all are sexually dimorphic. They can also be very sensitive to cold. Prior to the last half of the Twentieth Century, these lories were not often kept in captivity. The Wilhelmina Lorikeet, *Charmosyna wilhelmina*, is the smallest of all the lories at about five inches long and weighing about 20 grams; similar in size to a parrotlet. These birds are found throughout New Guinea. Most of the lories in this group are quite uncommon in aviculture; however, a few species are found in the United States.

In the United States, the most frequently encountered member of the *Charmosyna* genus is the Stella's Lorikeet, *C. p. goliathina*. This bird is most remarkable with its very long tail feathers. The length of a Stella's body is about seven inches and the tail feathers can add additional nine or ten inches to its total length. This bird comes in two color phases, red and melanistic. The red phase is dark on the back of its head, has green wings and the tail is green with yellow at the end. Its face, breast and abdomen are red. In the melanistic phase the red on the head and breast are replaced with black or almost black coloring. This is one of the lory species that is sexually dimorphic. In the red phase, the females have a yellow patch on the lower back while the males' backs and thighs are red. Female melanistic Stella's Lorikeets have green flanks and backs while the males do not. The Stella's Lorikeet is exceptionally elegant in its appearance but is not known for having good pet quality. In spite of the reputation of being unsuited to life as a pet, this bird is well established in aviculture and has on occasion made a charming and quiet companion. It is a popular aviary bird, showing up in the collections of many lory breeders in the United States and Europe. It is also the one bird in this genus that seems to be hardy enough to endure colder temperatures and the melanistic birds do not do well in very warm climates. Its native range includes high elevations in the mountains of New Guinea, right up to the tree line, some ten thousand feet or higher.

The Striated Lorikeet, *Charmosyna multistriata*, is rare in the Unites States and only slightly more common in Europe. It's a small, quiet bird and lacks some of the flashy coloring that lories are known for. Its body is green and the breast and neck are streaked with yellow, hence its name. It has an orange beak with a distinctive blue-gray coloring on the upper mandible. No more common in aviculture than the Striated Lorikeet is the Fairy Lorikeet, *Charmosyna pulchella*. This little bird is mostly red with green wings. The wild populations of both birds are considered stable.

The Cardinal Lory, *Chalcopsitta cardinalis*, is the most common lory in the Solomon Islands. It is a beautiful bird with plumage that, unusual for a lory, is primarily a rich, dark red. These lories existed in very small numers in the United States until 1999 when an additional forty-nine birds were imported, adding to the population. They arrived in Europe about nine years earlier. Cardinal Lories are every bit as interesting as others in the genus are; however, because they are les common in activity, very few are finding their way into the pet market. Those who have had the opportunity to work with and keep these birds are quite enchanted with their personality and intelligence.

The Red-flanked or Pleasing Lorikeet, *Charmosyna placentas*, appears in small numbers in aviculture in the United States. It is one of the few lories that are sexually dimorphic. This bird is sensitive to the cold. In the proper, temperate climate it does fairly well in aviaries. It remains relatively popular in Europe.

While the Duchess Lorikeet, *Charmosyna margarethae*, is currently unknown in American aviculture, there have been some efforts made to import it through the Solomon Island Parrot Consortium. Hopefully in the next few years, this bird will be available to American aviculturists. I think they must be really cool birds, just for their scientific name alone.

Duyvenbode's Lory. Photo by Richard Brancato

Eos

Birds belonging to the *Eos* genus include Red, Blue-streaked, Violet-naped Red-and-blue, Black-winged and the extremely uncommon Blue-eared Lories. The Red-and-blue Lory, *Eos histrio*, is one of the two lories listed on CITES Appendix I. All *Eos* lories are primarily bright red birds with dark blue or black markings and orange beaks. All the members of this group occupy islands in Indonesia. Red, Black-winged and Blue-streaked Lories are about eleven inches in length and on the average weigh 160 to 180 grams. Violet Naped lories are slightly smaller at about nine or ten inches and approximately 115 grams. Birds of the *Eos* genus are relatively hardy and adapt well to captivity.

One of the most common lories in American Aviculture is the Red Lory, *Eos bornea.* There are two types found in the U.S., the nominate species *E. b. bornea,* commonly called the Moluccan Red lory and the less common and slightly smaller subspecies *E. b. cyanonothus* or Buru Red Lory. As might be evident from their common names, the nominate species, the Moluccan Red, is native to the Moluccan Islands and the Buru native to the island of Buru. Red Lories are bright red birds with some blue on their sides. The wings are red with some dark blue or black. The area around the vent and under the tail is bright blue and their feet are dark. The Buru Red is slightly smaller in size and the red coloring is darker, almost maroon in some cases. Red Lories are popular in part because of their color and availability. My very first lory was a Red Lory and I was drawn to it because of the vibrant color and engaging personality. Red Lories have readily adapted to captivity and are known to be prolific breeders. They exist in large numbers throughout the United States. They can become accomplished talkers. Some who have kept both types have indicated there is a noticeable difference in the behavior and mannerisms of the two.

Blue-streaked Lories, *Eos reticulata,* are native to the Tanibar Islands of Indonesia where the population has been declining and their future is shaky at best. These birds are about the same size and shape as the Moluccan red but are easily distinguished by the amount of bright blue on their necks and ears. They also have some blue color streaked across their backs. Like the Red Lories, they are friendly and gregarious birds. Easy to breed, they have become one of the mainstays in the pet lory market. For a lory, they can often talk fairly well. While they appear in the United States in abundant quantities, their numbers in Europe have dwindled.

The Violet-naped or Violet-necked Lory, *Eos squamata*, is less common in the United States than the Red or the Blue-streaked Lory. They are more securely established in South Africa, Asia, and are commonly found in Europe. The slightly smaller Obi subspecies, *E. s. obiensis*, is not common in the United States but occurs with more frequency in Canada and Europe. The natural range of these birds includes the Moluccas and nearby islands.

Blue-eared, *E. semilarvata*, and Red-and-blue Lories, *E. histrio,* are known to have appeared in the United States but are not common and probably all but nonexistent at this time.

Glossopsitta

These are small birds from Australia. Lories in this family include the Musk, Purple-crowned and the Little Lorikeet. At one time the Goldie's Lorikeet was placed in this genus but it most commonly placed in the *Trichoglossus* genus. These birds are not often found in American aviculture. While the population in Australia is large, that country has strict regulations that prohibit the export of their birds. Of the three species in this genus, the Musk, *G. consinna,* is the only one that is likely to show up in U.S. aviculture. It is a pretty little green bird with a red streak behind the eyes and on the forehead. It seems to reproduce fairly well in captivity. As recently as the mid 1980s, Purple-crowned Lorikeets, *G. porphyrocephala*, were only rumored to exist in the United States. To what extent these birds are still being kept or if they are still being kept is not known. They are relatively common in Australian aviaries.

Lorius

This group contains some of the most commonly seen and kept lories in the United States and Europe. Members of the *Lorius* genus include the Chattering, Black-capped, Yellow-bibbed and Purple-naped. The birds in this genus are large and stocky with broad tails. They are primarily red with green wings and hail from New Guinea and some of its neighboring islands. They are about eleven inches long and all but the Yellow-bibbed lory generally weigh over 200 grams.

The Chattering Lory, *Lorius garrulus*, is a popular bird and makes for a good companion. There are two birds in this category, the nominate species, *Lorius garrulus*, and the subspecies commonly called the Yellow-backed Lory, *L. g. flavopallaitus*. The Yellow-backed Lory is different from the nominate species in the obvious patch of yellow on its mantle. Chattering Lories lack the black cap that is seen other *Lorius* species. They are active birds and many have been known to be accomplished talkers. They are well established in American and European aviculture. They are known for interacting well with humans and their outgoing personality makes them desirable as pets. They are forest dwelling birds of Indonesia. These birds still maintain a large wild population but it is on the decline as a result of their popularity as pets. According to BirdLife International, the Chattering Lory is the most popularly exported bird in Eastern Indonesia. They are popular in the United States and are one of the lories more commonly kept as pets in Europe.

The Black-capped Lory, *Lorius lory,* is another popular bird. Similar in size to the Chattering Lory, it has a black cap and varying amounts of blue on its breast or abdomen depending on which subspecies. These birds are known to be great companions and seem to adapt to and breed well

Blue-streaked Lory

in captivity. There are three known subspecies of this bird in the United States; the nominate species, *Lorius lory lory*, *L. lory salvadorii*, and *L. lory erythrothorax*. Black-capped Lories have bright red on their bodies, a black cap, and blue on the mantle and neck that extends down to the abdomen. The extent of the blue markings on the breast and abdomen varies according to subspecies. The ankles are bright blue. The wings are green and feathers under the wings have a patch of yellow which shows clearly when the bird flies. Their beaks are orange and their legs are black.

Black-capped Lories

Gaining in popularity and numbers in the United States and Europe is the Yellow-bibbed Lory, *Lorius chlorocercus*. With the exception of only a handful of birds, the Yellow-bibbed Lory was practically unknown in the United States until 1998. At that time, it was imported through the

Solomon Island Parrot Consortium. It was imported into Europe several years earlier. It is the smallest of the *Lorius* genus at ten to eleven inches in length and weighing about 170 grams. It is a red bird with green wings and a black crown. Its shoulders are pale blue and its thighs and underwings are bright, deep blue. Its most remarkable characteristic is the wide yellow collar, or "bib" around its neck. Those who have had the chance to work with this bird have found that it breeds readily in captivity and makes a delightful companion. Because of the breeding success in the United States, the Yellow-bibbed Lory is well on its way to becoming an avicultural mainstay.

Less commonly seen in American and European aviculture is the Purple-naped or Purple-capped Lory, *Lorius domicellus*. This bird has a red body, green wings, a yellow collar and its black cap turns into purple towards the nape. It has some distinctive vocalizations, most of which are delivered loudly. It comes from the islands of Seram and Ambon; however, it may no longer even exist on Ambon. As the inhabitant of small islands, its population was never strong and is rapidly decreasing, estimated to be currently less than 10,000 birds. The decline in numbers is primarily due to habitat destruction. There are local laws to protect the bird but it seems they are rarely enforced. This bird is not well represented in aviculture. It is reputed to be rather difficult to breed and is not well established in the United States. Only a handful of these birds were imported in the late 1980s to about 1990. There are several in

Purple-naped Lory

private collections and in a handful of zoos. It does occur a bit more often in collections in Europe. I have had the good fortune to have a pair of these birds. They have turned out to be prolific egg layers although more often than not the eggs are infertile. Although incredibly curious and very aggressive birds, they have the type of charming personality that would make them suitable companion birds.

Neopsittacus

The two lories in this group are the Musschenbroek's or Yellow-billed and the Emerald Lorikeet. These birds frequent the higher elevations of New Guinea and their diet has more variation than most other lory species. Both of these birds were introduced into U.S. aviculture but are rarely seen now. Because they are perceived by many as having poor pet quality, the market for them is limited.

While not terribly popular in the United States, Musschenbroek's Lorikeets, *Neopsittacus musschenbroekii,* have done well in European aviculture. They are small, green birds with bright red breasts. While they seem to breed readily in captivity, they tend to be nippy and ill suited to life as a pet. They do well in aviaries with mixed species and tend not to be aggressive with non-lory birds.

Oreopsittacus

The only bird classified in this genus is the Whiskered Lorikeet, *Oreopsittacus arfaki.* It is not a bird commonly seen in aviculture although it shows up occasionally in a zoo or private collection. The Whiskered Lorikeet has the unique trait of having fourteen tail feathers as opposed to the twelve found on other parrots. It is also sexually dimorphic, meaning the genders are distinctly different from one another. The Whiskered Lorikeet is naturally found high in the mountains of Irian Jaya, New Guinea.

Phigys

The only member of this genus, the Collared or Solitary lory, *Phigys solitarus,* is considered by many taxonomists to be a member of the *Vini* genus. This is a beautiful bird with a dark purple crown, forehead, thighs and lower abdomen, red abdomen and green mantle, wings and tail. It inhabits Fiji and rarely occurs in captivity. The San Diego Zoo has had success breeding these birds.

Pseudeos

Pseudeos is another monotypic genus; the only member is the Dusky Lory, *Pseudeos fuscata*. Dusky Lories are native to New Guinea, commonly found all over, from forests in higher elevations to lowland savannahs. They are migratory birds and can often be found with groups of other lories. This "dressed-for-Halloween" bird comes in two color phases, yellow and orange. The beak and eyes are orange. The body is generally dark brown with orange or yellow on the head, throat and abdomen. Duskies are one of the most popular pet lories and they make playful and talkative companions. They are about ten inches long and weigh about 150 to 160 grams. This makes them the perfect size for a companion. Their chirps and squawks can be quite loud and high-pitched and they can be quite aggressive and stubborn. When discussing their personality, Dusky Lories have at times been referred to as the "Extreme Lory" or "lories squared. Traits, behaviors and antics that are typically ascribed to lories seem to be taken to the extreme with Dusky lories. They are intense little birds. They have adapted well to captivity and breed prolifically. They are common in aviaries throughout the United States and Europe.

Psitteuteles

This genus has included such birds as the Goldie's, Iris and Varied Lorikeet. To underscore how inexact taxonomy is, the genus is recognized by some and not by others. In *Parrots of the World*, Forshaw disregarded it and classified these birds with *Trichoglossus*; however, Juniper and Parr do not. In his 1896 text, Mivart placed the Goldie's Lorikeet with *Glossopsitta*. For the purposes of this book, I will follow the classification established by Forshaw and list these birds in the genus *Trichoglossus*.

Trichoglossus

Genus *Trichoglossus* has several popular lory species including the Rainbow Lories. Lories are undoubtedly some of the most beautiful birds in the world, and none stand out more than the popular and appropriately named Rainbow lories. Rainbow lories range from about nine to eleven inches in length and 95 to 130 grams in weight. These widely distributed birds are native to Australia and many of the Islands of Indonesia and the South Pacific. For the most part they exist in their natural environments in great numbers; however, on a few of the islands the habitat is diminishing and there may be some cause for concern. They have been heavily traded and over the years have achieved great popularity as pets and household companions. The term "Rainbow Lory" is a generic one applied to over twenty separate brightly colored types of birds. These birds have similar yet distinct coloration. They tend to have green bodies, blue heads, and yellow, orange, or red breasts. The Rainbow group, *Trichoglossus haematodus,* is comprised of one nominate species, commonly called the Green-naped Lory, and approximately twenty-two subspecies. Of this group about eight subspecies appear, or have appeared at some point, in American aviculture.

The Green-naped Lory, the nominate species *T. h. haematodus,* is by the far the most commonly seen and most readily available bird in this group. It is easy to breed and appears frequently in the pet trade. Green-naped Lories mainly inhabit the islands of New Guinea and Indonesia where it is plentiful and often appears in large flocks at the forest's edge. Its body is green and the forehead, crown and lores are blue, shaft streaked with green. The back of its head is purple; the breast is red with the feathers clearly edged in dark blue. The collar is greenish yellow. While extremely popular as pets, this bird has a reputation for becoming nippy when mature.

Another popular and commonly seen member of this family is the Swainson's or Blue-mountain Lory, *T. h. molluccanus.* Its head is dark blue to violet, shaft streaked with a lighter blue. The abdomen is dark blue and the breast is orange and does not have the dark tipped feathers seen on the Green-naped Lory. The collar is yellow-green. Several color mutations have been documented but they are extremely rare. This lory is native to Eastern Australia where it can be seen frequently in yards and other populated areas.

The Edward's Lory, *T. h. capistratus*, is becoming more common and in my opinion has the nicest temperament of the entire group. The body is green. The head is green; the forehead, crown, and chin are blue, shaft streaked with a darker blue. The breast is yellow with a bit of orange edging, the abdomen is dark green and the collar is a greenish yellow. This bird is native to the lowlands of Timor. In general, the Edward's Lory seems to be less nippy and aggressive than the Green-naped Lory when mature. This increases its desirability as a pet.

The remaining five species, including the Rosenberg's or Biak Lory (*T. h. rosenbergii*), Blue-headed or Pale-headed Lory (*T. h. caeruleiceps*), and the Weber's Lory (*T. h. weberi*) appear less frequently in this country. The Weber's is the only lory of the rainbow group not as brilliantly colored. It is mainly green and yellow. The slightly smaller Mitchell's Lory, *T. h. mitchellii*, has almost completely disappeared from aviculture in the United States and all that remains here now is a fragile population. Additionally, the wild population in its native home on the islands of Bali and Lombak appears to have diminished significantly and the existing population is in peril. Forsten's Lories (*T. h. forsteni*) were imported into the U.S. periodically in the past but have become scarce in recent years. Its status in the wild is believed to be declining as well. There may be a few specimens of some of the other Rainbow subspecies still in the United States but they are almost unheard of and, with no apparent viable population, they are rarely seen.

Green-naped Lory. Photo by Kristen Bliss

The *Trichoglossus* family has some fun non-rainbow species as well. One small and very fun little bird is the Goldie's Lorikeet, *Trichoglossus goldiei*. This bird is generally assigned to the genus Trichoglossus as indicated in popular texts such as Joseph Forshaw's "Parrots of the World" and Rosemary Low's "Encyclopedia of Lories"; however, other texts place it in the genus *Psitteuteles*. This lory will remind you of a watermelon with its green streaked body and red forehead and crown and purple face. It is about seven inches long and weighs between 50 and 80 grams. It is native to the mountains of New Guinea where it is still fairly common. These diminutive birds make delightful companions and are considered by many to be a good lory for a beginner. They are the complete lory spirit in a small package but they are not known to be exceptionally good talkers. Not only do they make wonderful pets, they also do well in mixed aviaries. Their popularity in the United States is growing. In Europe they are grabbed up as soon as they become available because their numbers there have been depleted.

Another delightful member of this genus is the Iris Lory, *T. iris*. This bird is from Timor and is vulnerable there as the habit is rapidly disappearing. Iris Lories are small, about 8 inches long. They have red crowns, a band of purple behind their eyes, yellow scalloping on their breast, and green bodies. Iris Lories have a more varied diet than other lories. Often they are fed a small parrot seed mix along with fruit and nectar. They are one of the few lories known to aviculture that do well with some seeds in their diet. Iris Lories are appearing more often as companion birds. They are not terribly noisy and have charming dispositions, which makes them well suited for life with humans.

The Scaly-breasted Lory, *Trichoglossus chlorolepidotus*, is a small, bright green bird with a yellow scalloped breast and bright orange under the wings. It comes from Australia and is about nine inches long, weighing about 75 grams. It has a rather melodious voice, if any lory voice can be considered melodious. They are commonly kept in Australia, where several natural mutations have occurred. In the United States they do not enjoy the same popularity as other members of the *Trichoglossus* genus and are becoming quite uncommon.

The Yellow-and-green Lories, *Trichoglossus flavoviridis*, are not kept in the US, but there are established populations in Europe, South Africa, and Asia.

Vini

Lories in the *Vini* genus are small colorful birds with short tails. They are native to places not known for other parrot species such as Tahiti, Fiji, and the Marquesas. This group of delicate little birds includes the Tahitian Blue, Aquamarine, Blue-crowned and the Kuhl's Lory. Birds in this group occupy small island habitats and therefore do not exist naturally in huge numbers. Their fragile populations are declining every day due to rats, pesticides, and habitat destruction. They occur only rarely in aviculture. In the United States, the San Diego Zoo has a few specimens of the Tahitian Blue, *Vini peruviana*. They were successful in breeding them, so much so that some were even passed along to the private sector. Unfortunately, due to Salmonella, only a few birds remain and they are old and no longer productive. In England, the Duke of Bedford had some success breeding it in the 1930s. Rosemary Low was able to rear some in her collection in the 1970s and 1980s. The Tahitian Blue Lory is actually believed to be extinct in Tahiti with only a small population remaining on the Society Islands and Cook Islands. Outside of its natural habitat in Rimitara there is only one known specimen of the Kuhl's Lory, *Vini kuhlii*. He is part of a private collection in Southern California.

Drawing by Mark Ziembicki

Vini ultramarina, the Ultramarine Lory, is one of two lories listed on appendix I of CITES. Native to the Marquesas, the Ultramarine lory population has diminished significantly due primarily to the introduction of rats to the islands it has occupied. This dramatically beautiful bird has been the object of attempts to relocate it to Fatu Hiva, a nearby island that was free of the rats that disrupt the nests. The efforts appeared to have some success and the number of birds increased in the new location, however it was discovered that rats have come to those islands as well and threatened the flock. Efforts are underway to control the rat populations without negatively impacting the environment. Current research has shown the island of Ua Huka to be rat free while hosting approximately 98% of the world's population of this little bird. It is believed that this population is the result of the introduction of a single pair in the 1940s. Research indicates that as of 2003, the estimated population is approximately 2300 birds. Continued efforts to keep rats off the island, coupled with the addition of artificial nests, along with the knowledge gained through research into its diet and habits, will hopefully allow this small population to grow and flourish.

The Blue-crowned Lory, *Vini australis*, is the only lory of this genus that is found in private aviculture in the United States. It is about seven inches long and weighs 35 to 45 grams. This little bird is bright green with a red bib that extends down from its eyes to its neck. It has a red or purplish patch on the abdomen and a bright blue crown. While quite beautiful, this is not an easy bird to breed. They tend to be quite aggressive towards one another. Aggression, their relatively few numbers, and their high price are why they are not considered to be well suited to life as a pet.

References

Australian Parrots; Joseph M. Forshaw, Alexander Editions, Third Revised Edition, 2002

Avian Medicine, Principles and Applications; Ritchie, Harrison and Harrison, Wingers Publishing, 1994

Birds in Papua New Guinea; Brian J. Coates, Robert Brown & Associates, 1977

Comparative Avian Nutrition; Kirk Klasing, CAB International, New York, 1998.

A Guide to Lories & Lorikeet; Peter Odekerken, Australian Birdkeeper, 1995

Hancock House Encyclopedia of the Lories; Rosemary Low, Hancock House, 1998

Lories; Michael W. Gos, T.F.H Publications, 1981

Lories & Lorikeets; Rosemary Low, Van Nostrand Reinhold Company, 1977

Lories & Lorikeets; Alison Ruggles, Blandford, 1995

Parrots; A Guide to Parrots of the World; Tony Juniper and Mike Parr, Yale University Press, 1998

Parrots: Handfeeding and Nursery Management; Howard Voren and Rick Jordan, Silvio Mattacchione & Co., 1993

Parrots and Parrot-Like Birds; Duke of Bedford, All-Pets Books, 1954

Parrot Family Birds; Julien L. Bronson, All-Pets Magazine, 1950

Parrots of the World; Joseph M. Forshaw, Doubleday & Company, Inc., 1973

Psittacine Aviculture; Schubot, Clubb and Clubb, ABRC; Willis Printing Group, 1992

The Loriidae. A Monograph of the Lories or brush-tongued Parrots composing the family Loriidae; St. George Mivart, 1896

Merriam Webster's Collegiate Dictionary; Tenth Edition, 1993

PAPERS

The Asian Vulture Crisis; The Peregrine Fund; www.peregrinefund.org/conserv_vulture.html

Basic Avian Clinical Pathology Testing; Heidi L. Hoefer, DVM, Dip ABVP-Avian Practice, West Hills Animal HospitalHuntington, New York, 2003

Common Infectious Diseases of Psittacine Birds; Branson Ritchie DVM, ABVP, November 2003 presentation.

Experimental Transmission of Psittacine Proventricular Dilatation Disease (PDD) and Preliminary Characterization of a Virus Recovered From Birds With Naturally Occurring and Experimentally Induced PDD; Christopher R. Gregory, Branson W. Ritchie, Kenneth S. Latimer, W. L. Steffens, Raymond P. Campagnoli, Denise Pesti, and Phil D. Lukert, College of Veterinary Medicine, The University of Georgia, Proceedings from the International Virtual Conferences in Veterinary Medicine, 1998

Hemochromatosis in Lories; Margrethe Warden, 2001

Jewels Lost in an Ocean: The Plight of the Vini Lorikeets in the South Pacidic Islands; Mark Ziembicki, American Lory Society *Network*, Volume 8, Number III, 2001

Keeping Lories in a Colony; Jos Hubers, Lory Journal International, Issue 1, 2003

Lories as Pets; Margrethe Warden, Lory Journal International, Issue 1, 2001

Rainbow Lories In American Aviculture; Margrethe Warden, 2002

Reducing Behavior Problems in Lories and Lorikeets; Hans Hovens , Lory Journal International, Issue 3, 2001

Status, distribution and conservation of the Ultramarine lorikeet Vini ultramarina in the Marquesas Islands, French Polynesia; Marc Ziembicki and Philippe Raust, School of Earth and Environmental Sciences University of Adelaide, December 2003

Visceral Gout in Birds; Margrethe Warden, 2003

What Is Aviculture; Margrethe Warden 2004

White House Pets; Roger Segelken, Cornell University Science News, 1997

WEB

BirdLife International – www.birdlife.net

Centers for Disease Control and Prevention (CDC) –www.cdc.gov

Convention on International Trade in Endangered Species – www.cites.org

International Species Information System - www.isis.org

PERSONAL COMMUNICATION

Cheryl Greenacre DVM, ABVP Dilpomate, Formerly of the University of Georgia, now University of Tennessee

Branson Ritchie DVM, PhD, ABVP Diplomate, University of Georgia

Heather Wilson DVM, ABVP Diplomate, University of Georgia

Mary Chinnici

Dick Schroeder

Matt Schmit

Penny Solgot

Donna Lynn Salyer

Devorah Bennu

Fred Wilson

Index

A

AAV ...*87*

accidents ...*111*, *134*

anthropomorphism ...60

aspergillosis ...*21*, *39*, *89*, *102*

avian veterinarian ...*118*

avocado ...*35*, *125*

B

bacteria ...*30*, *47*, *51*, *53*, *89*, *96*, *103*, *107*, *110*, *124*

bar spacing ...*26*, *39*

bathing ...*44*, *49*

beak and feather disease ...*21*, *89*, *103*

beak trimming ...*118*

behavior
...*36*, *54*, *57*, 60, *62*, 76, *86*, *88*, *96*, *99*, *141*, *158*, *166*

biting ...36, *55*, *62*, 140

Black Lories ...*152*

Black-capped Lories ...*68*, *78*, *160*, 161

Printed in the United States
20599LVS00001B/196-339